High School Kickers Off-Season Training Program

January through July

By Coach Bill Renner

Training Thesis Statement

It is my belief that anyone can be trained to perform the skill of kicking as long as they are performing the right skill techniques that will produce the desired results.

It is my belief, which has been successfully proven by researchers and my own independent study as a long time football coach, that people and kickers do not realize their potential because they do not do the right drills and do not perform enough training repetitions.

The **Kickers Off-Season Training Program** overcomes both of those obstacles. It gives you the right drills to perform and the right number of repetitions to enable you to develop to your full potential.

It also correctly coordinates the sequencing of weight lifting and running training with the kicking training so that you can improve physically and transfer that to successful kicking.

This program is not happenstance. It is the result of over 25 years of developing kicking training methodology through actually coaching kickers that were part of the teams I coached, in a camp or individual setting.

It is the culmination of having coached a wide range of kicking talent and developing a program that can be used by the beginner or advanced. This proves to be true because it is a skill that is being honed and a person that is being trained.

Skill techniques are consistent and absolute and the training and conditioning goal for the player is always to be in peak performance for the season, two criteria taken into account with the design of this program. Thus, talent level is not a criterion when designing a training program; however, strengths and weaknesses are.

This kicking training program provides enough skill drills to change mechanic weaknesses to strengths and simulates enough game situation repetitions to change performance weaknesses into strengths providing the focus, intensity and commitment to doing each rep correctly is adhered to.

Good luck with your training.

Coach Bill Renner

BEFORE you start, know this:

HOW will this training program work:

when **long term commitment** combines with **high levels of practice**

WHAT is your role:

"It's all about their (your) perception of (your) self."

"What ignited the process wasn't any innate skill or gene. It was a small…yet powerful idea: a vision of their ideal future selves, a vision that oriented, energized and accelerated progress and that originated in the outside world."

pg. 104-105, *The Talent Code*, Dan Coyle

High School Kickers Off-Season Training Program

To maximize kicking ability, a kicking workout program must consist of flexibility, agilities, strength training, running and a kicking specific workout program. The most important of these areas is the kicking specific workout program.

The best time period to develop and sharpen your kicking technique is in the off-season, specifically from January through July. During this time period you can adjust your mechanics without affecting your performance since there are no games. This is the time to work on your technique flaws that you had from the past season and to learn to be more mechanically efficient.

You will become stronger and more powerful from the strength program and running program which will help the height and distance of your kicks. However, these gains will have no positive effect on your performance during the season if you do not improve your technique. How well the techniques of kicking are performed is what separates the average kickers from the good ones. It is also the key to being a consistent, dependable performer.

The first phase of this kicking training program starts in January and progresses through July when summer football practice starts.

The emphasis during this time frame is on technique development. Regardless of the level of proficiency you have achieved, a period of technique evaluation and development is needed. In fact, no area of a year round training program is as essential toward maximizing your ability as this technique period.

Proper technique is the foundation for being a consistent and effective performer. Taking a period of time to hone the fundamentals which need to be performed to successfully execute the skill of kicking is the proper way to begin.

January through March begins the technique development phase of the program. _In order to emphasize technique you should not kick outside during this phase_. All kicking during the first three months is to be done into a net. Most kickers have never done this before, but it is important for you to learn not to judge your success as a kicker by the flight of or the result of the ball's travel.

Most coaches and kickers will look at the flight or result of the ball and see a fifty-yard field goal and think that the kicker is good. However, you may have technique faults and still be able to accomplish those type of kicks. The error in this evaluation procedure is that without proper technique you cannot perform those kicks on command or when you need to in a game. Typically, these are your good practice kickers but poor game performers. You look good in practice but do not make the same kind of kicks in the game.

The other component which needs to be incorporated when you are only kicking into a net is videotape analysis. Just as other position groups are analyzed for proper steps, body position and general technique of their positions, you also need to analyze yourself for proper technique. The saying that "the big eye in the sky (camera) does not lie" holds true for kickers also.

My previous book, _Kicking the Football_, will enable you to know what the basic mechanics of the kick are so that you can completely and confidently evaluate yourself on the video. Videotaping and evaluation should be done twice a week the first month, January, of the training and once a week during February and March. From April through July you should videotape twice a month as a minimum or when needed. For example, you may not be kicking well and do not know what you are doing wrong. This would be a good time to videotape yourself the next couple of kicking workouts and watch it to fix your errors.

Twice a week videotape analysis for the first month will enable you to establish a level of proficiency or change any bad technique habits that you had during the season. Start by focusing on one or two techniques adjustments a week and continue evaluating those until you have eliminated them from your technique. Keep a list of all the things you need to change in your technique, but make a second list of an implementation schedule for when to work on them.

Always do the warm-up drills, quick feet drills, prior to kicking. These are not only designed for warming-up but are valuable in working on technique. Your leg muscle has no idea when it swings whether it makes contact with a ball or not. The ball's weight is too insignificant to affect energy expenditure. So in addition to working on a part of the skill before doing the whole skill the drills enable you to get swings in without having to kick the football. This permits multiple reps in a shorter period of time and "perfect practice makes perfect".

There is a day in between the kicking workout days during this phase. You will be lifting and running on these days so it will not be a total day of rest. But the kicking specific movement muscles need a rest day in between kicking workout days to recover so don't be tempted to punt every day just follow the program.

On the kicking workout days, you will also do the running workout. You should always do the kicking workout before the running workout. While kicking is an explosive, strenuous activity the muscular energy system you use to kick will be replenished quicker than the demands running places on the muscular energy system. Thus, the kicking workout will not affect the running workout.

This does not work the other way however; doing the running work before the kicking workout can have a negative effect on the punting workout. Fatigue and lack of muscular recovery will affect your techniques and hinder the objective of this training phase which is to develop proper technique. So, kick before you do the running workout.

Expert Development
Training Formula

deep practice X 10,000 hours = world-class skill

"<u>deep practice</u> is built on a paradox: struggling in certain targeted ways – operating at the edges of your ability, where you make mistakes – makes you smarter. …experiences where you're forced to slow down, make errors, and correct them….end up making you swift and graceful without your realizing it." pg. 18, *The Talent Code,* Dan Coyle

"<u>Skills</u> consists of identifying important elements and grouping them into a meaningful framework." (chunking) pg. 77, *The Talent Code,* Dan Coyle

"…<u>experts practice differently</u> and far more strategically. When they fail, they don't blame it on luck or themselves. They have a strategy they can fix." pg. 85, *The Talent Code*, Barry Zimmerman, City University of New York, Professor of Psychology

"<u>Attentive repetition</u>…Nothing you can do…is more effective in building skill than executing the action, firing the impulse down the nerve fiber, fixing errors, honing the circuit." pg. 87, *The Talent Code,* Dan Coyle

High School Kickers Off-Season Monthly Training Emphasis

Month	Body	Leg	Kicking	Strategy
January	core stability	leg endurance	movements	technique
February	core stability	leg endurance	movements	technique
March	core stability	leg endurance	movements	technique
April	core explosion	swing control	short field goals	winning FG's
May	core explosion	leg strength	long field goals	long range
June	core execution	leg recovery	flight control	mental control
July	core execution	leg recovery	refine technique	preseason prep

Training Program Notes

Power in the body, strength and speed, comes from having a strong core of hips, thighs, and butt muscles. The weight lifting exercises are designed around developing these areas. The exercises are not age dependent but the amount of weight used and training emphasis is. Use the following table as a guide.

Age	Training Emphasis	Weight
10-13	correct lifting form	moderate – be able to do 2 more reps than prescribed
14-18	strength	*heavy – be able to do only the prescribed reps
		*add 5 lbs of weight when you can complete all the reps

High School KICKERS
OFF-SEASON Training Calendar
Total Reps

Month	Quick Feet Repetitions	Net Kicking Repetitions	Field Goal Reps	Game Winning Field Goal Workouts	Long Distance Field Goal Workouts
January	160	200	0	0	0
February	160	200	0	0	0
March	175	325	0	0	0
April	140	0	325	12	0
May	145	0	325	0	12
June	160	0	325	7	7
July	145	0	140	8	0
Totals	1,080	725	1,115	28	19

January

Workout Charts

High School KICKERS
OFF-SEASON Training Calendar
January

SUNDAY	MONDAY	TUESDAY	WEDNESDAY	THURSDAY	FRIDAY	SATURDAY
Week 1 NO WORKOUT REST	Week 1 **Kickers** Quick Feet Drills Weightlifting	Week 1 **Kick** 25 reps into net Ball Contact Kicking Workout Running Workout	Week 1 **Kickers** Quick Feet Drills Weightlifting	Week 1 **Kick** 25 reps into net Ball Contact Kicking Workout Running Workout	Week 1 **Kickers** Quick Feet Drills Weightlifting	Week 1 No training prescribed rest or participate in light physical activity. i.e. basketball, biking, etc.
Week 2 NO WORKOUT REST	Week 2 **Kickers** Quick Feet Drills Weightlifting	Week 2 **Kick** 25 reps into net Ball Contact Kicking Workout Running Workout	Week 2 **Kickers** Quick Feet Drills Weightlifting	Week 2 **Kick** 25 reps into net Ball Contact Kicking Workout Running Workout	Week 2 **Kickers** Quick Feet Drills Weightlifting	Week 2 No training prescribed rest or participate in light physical activity. i.e. basketball, biking, etc.
Week 3 NO WORKOUT REST	Week 3 **Kickers** Quick Feet Drills Weightlifting	Week 3 **Kick** 25 reps into net Ball Contact Kicking Workout Running Workout	Week 3 **Kickers** Quick Feet Drills Weightlifting	Week 3 **Kick** 25 reps into net Ball Contact Kicking Workout Running Workout	Week 3 **Kickers** Quick Feet Drills Weightlifting	Week 3 No training prescribed rest or participate in light physical activity. i.e. basketball, biking, etc.
Week 4 NO WORKOUT REST	Week 4 **Kickers** Quick Feet Drills Weightlifting	Week 4 **Kick** 25 reps into net Ball Contact Kicking Workout Running Workout	Week 4 **Kickers** Quick Feet Drills Weightlifting	Week 4 **Kick** 25 reps into net Ball Contact Kicking Workout Running Workout	Week 4 **Kickers** Quick Feet Drills Weightlifting	Week 4 No training prescribed rest or participate in light physical activity. i.e. basketball, biking, etc.

High School KICKERS
OFF-SEASON SPEED and STRENGTH Training Program
January

MONDAY	TUESDAY	WEDNESDAY	THURSDAY	FRIDAY
Flexibility Agility Warm-up Dynamic Flexibility ------------------ **Kicker Drills** **1 set of 10** No Step Drill One Step Drill Quick Feet Full Approach Drill ------------------ **Core Lifts** **3 sets of 8** Squat Close Grip Bench Press ------------------ **Auxiliary Lifts** **2 sets of 8** Lat Pull Front Raises Lateral Raises Arm Curls Tricep Extension	**Flexibility** Agility Warm-up Dynamic Flexibility ------------------ **Kicker Drills** **1 set of 5** No Step Drill One Step Drill Quick Feet Full Approach Drill ------------------ **Kicking Workout** 25 Kicks into the NET ------------------ **Running Workout** 3 x 440 yds – 1:30 sec each 3 minute rest between each	**Flexibility** Agility Warm-up Dynamic Flexibility ------------------ **Kicker Drills** **1 set of 10** No Step Drill One Step Drill Quick Feet Full Approach Drill ------------------ **Core Lifts** **3 sets of 8** Cleans Deadlift ------------------ **Auxiliary Lifts** **2 sets of 8** Glute Ham Raise Push Press Dips	**Flexibility** Agility Warm-up Dynamic Flexibility ------------------ **Kicker Drills** **1 set of 5** No Step Drill One Step Drill Quick Feet Full Approach Drill ------------------ **Kicking Workout** 25 Kicks into the NET ------------------ **Running Workout** 3 x 440 yds – 1:30 sec each 3 minute rest between each	**Flexibility** Agility Warm-up Dynamic Flexibility ------------------ **Kicker Drills** **1 set of 10** No Step Drill One Step Drill Quick Feet Full Approach Drill ------------------ **Core Lifts** **3 sets of 8** Lunges Bench Press ------------------ **Auxiliary Lifts** **2 sets of 8** Lat Pulls Leg Extension Leg Curls Neck Arm Curls Tricep Extension

Agility Warm-up Routine
*15 yards – down and back using each movement
High knees
Shuffle
Carioca
Backpedal
Butt kicks
Power skips
Sprint

Dynamic Flexibility Routine
*10 yards—down and back using each movement
Tin soldiers
Walking Hamstring
Knee Tuck/Quad Pull
Front Lunges
Back Lunges
Spiderman

Kicker Workout Recording Sheet

Monday
January Week 1

Flexibility   ### Check when completed

Agility Warm-up   _____
*high knees, shuffle, carioca, backpedal, butt kicks, power skips, spring

Dynamic Flexibility   _____
*tin man, walking hamstring, knee tuck/quad pull, front lunges, back lunges, spiderman

Kicking Without the Ball Drills   ### Check when completed

Quick Feet Full Approach Swings	1 x 10 swings	_____
One-Step Swings	1 x 10 swings	_____
No-Step Swings	1 x 10 swings	_____

Core Lifts   ### Weight Used

Squats	3 x 8 reps	_____
Close Grip Bench Press	3 x 8 reps	_____

Auxiliary Lifts   ### Weight Used

Lat Pulls	2 x 8 reps	_____
Front Raises (shoulders)	2 x 8 reps	_____
Lateral Raises (shoulders)	2 x 8 reps	_____
Arm Curls	2 x 8 reps	_____
Triceps Extensions	2 x 8 reps	_____

Notes
1) Use a weight you can complete all the repetitions comfortably meaning you could do one or two more at the end of the set.
2) When you could do more than two more repetitions on a set move the weight used up 5 pounds.
3) Rest only 1 minute between sets and no longer.

Kicker Workout Recording Sheet

Tuesday
January Week 1

Flexibility   Check when completed

Agility Warm-up   _____
*high knees, shuffle, carioca, backpedal, butt kicks, power skips, spring

Dynamic Flexibility   _____
*tin man, walking hamstring, knee tuck/quad pull, front lunges, back lunges, spiderman

Kicking With the Ball Drills   Check when completed

Quick Feet Full Approach Swings   1 x 5 swings   _____

One-Step Swings   1 x 5 swings   _____

No-Step Swings   1 x 5 swings   _____

Kicking With the Ball Drills   Check when completed

At-the-Upright Drill (no step)   5 kicks   _____

Over-the-Upright Drill (one step)   5 kicks   _____

Down-the-Sideline Right sideline (full approach) 5 kicks _____

30 yard field goals middle   10 kicks   _____

Running Workout   Time of Run

3 x 440 yard run   1 minute 30 seconds for each run
                                                  3 minutes rest in between each run

Run 1: 440 yards   _____

Run 2: 440 yards   _____

Run 3: 440 yards   _____

Notes
1) Use a weight you can complete all the repetitions comfortably meaning you could do one or two more at the end of the set.
2) When you could do more than two more repetitions on a set move the weight used up 5 pounds.
3) Rest only 1 minute between sets and no longer.

Kicker Workout Recording Sheet

Wednesday
January Week 1

Flexibility   Check when completed

Agility Warm-up   _____
*high knees, shuffle, carioca, backpedal, butt kicks, power skips, spring

Dynamic Flexibility   _____
*tin man, walking hamstring, knee tuck/quad pull, front lunges, back lunges, spiderman

Kicking Without the Ball Drills   Check when completed

Quick Feet Full Approach Swings   1 x 10 swings   _____

One-Step Swings   1 x 10 swings   _____

No-Step Swings   1 x 10 swings   _____

Core Lifts   Weight Used

Power Cleans   3 x 8 reps   _____

Deadlift   3 x 8 reps   _____

Auxiliary Lifts   Weight Used

Glute Ham Raise   2 x 8 reps   _____

Push Press   2 x 8 reps   _____

Dips   2 x 8 reps   _____

Notes
1) Use a weight you can complete all the repetitions comfortably meaning you could do one or two more at the end of the set.
2) When you could do more than two more repetitions on a set move the weight used up 5 pounds.
3) Rest only 1 minute between sets and no longer.

Kicker Workout Recording Sheet

Thursday
January Week 1

Flexibility   ### Check when completed

Agility Warm-up   _____
*high knees, shuffle, carioca, backpedal, butt kicks, power skips, spring

Dynamic Flexibility   _____
*tin man, walking hamstring, knee tuck/quad pull, front lunges, back lunges, spiderman

Kicking Without the Ball Drills   ### Check when completed

Quick Feet Full Approach Swings   1 x 5 swings   _____

One-Step Swings   1 x 5 swings   _____

No-Step Swings   1 x 5 swings   _____

Kicking With the Ball Drills   ### Check when completed

At-the-Upright Drill (no step)   5 kicks   _____

Over-the-Upright Drill)one step)   5 kicks   _____

Down-the-Sideline Right sideline (full approach) 5 kicks _____

30 yard field goals middle   10 kicks   _____

Running Workout   ### Time of Run

3 x 440 yard run   1 minute 30 seconds for each run
                                      3 minutes rest in between each run

Run 1: 440 yards   _____

Run 2: 440 yards   _____

Run 3: 440 yards   _____

Notes
1) Use a weight you can complete all the repetitions comfortably meaning you could
   do one or two more at the end of the set.
2) When you could do more than two more repetitions on a set move the weight used up 5 pounds.
3) Rest only 1 minute between sets and no longer.

Kicker Workout Recording Sheet

Friday
January Week 1

Flexibility   Check when completed

Agility Warm-up   _____
*high knees, shuffle, carioca, backpedal, butt kicks, power skips, spring

Dynamic Flexibility   _____
*tin man, walking hamstring, knee tuck/quad pull, front lunges, back lunges, spiderman

Kicking Without the Ball Drills   Check when completed

Quick Feet Full Approach Swings	1 x 10 swings	_____
One-Step Swings	1 x 10 swings	_____
No-Step Swings	1 x 10 swings	_____

Core Lifts   Weight Used

Lunges	3 x 8 reps	_____
Bench Press	3 x 8 reps	_____

Auxiliary Lifts   Weight Used

Lat Pulls	2 x 8 reps	_____
Leg Extension	2 x 8 reps	_____
Leg Curls	2 x 8 reps	_____
Neck	2 x 8 reps	_____
Arm Curls	2 x 8 reps	_____
Triceps Extensions	2 x 8 reps	_____

Notes
1) Use a weight you can complete all the repetitions comfortably meaning you could do one or two more at the end of the set.
2) When you could do more than two more repetitions on a set move the weight used up 5 pounds.
3) Rest only 1 minute between sets and no longer

Kicker Workout Recording Sheet

Monday
January Week 2

Flexibility   Check when completed

Agility Warm-up   _____
*high knees, shuffle, carioca, backpedal, butt kicks, power skips, spring

Dynamic Flexibility   _____
*tin man, walking hamstring, knee tuck/quad pull, front lunges, back lunges, spiderman

Kicking Without the Ball Drills   Check when completed

Quick Feet Full Approach Swings	1 x 10 swings	_____
One-Step Swings	1 x 10 swings	_____
No-Step Swings	1 x 10 swings	_____

Core Lifts   Weight Used

Squats	3 x 8 reps	_____
Close Grip Bench Press	3 x 8 reps	_____

Auxiliary Lifts   Weight Used

Lat Pulls	2 x 8 reps	_____
Front Raises (shoulders)	2 x 8 reps	_____
Lateral Raises (shoulders)	2 x 8 reps	_____
Arm Curls	2 x 8 reps	_____
Triceps Extensions	2 x 8 reps	_____

Notes
1) Use a weight you can complete all the repetitions comfortably meaning you could do one or two more at the end of the set.
2) When you could do more than two more repetitions on a set move the weight used up 5 pounds.
3) Rest only 1 minute between sets and no longer.

Kicker Workout Recording Sheet

Tuesday
January Week 2

Flexibility   ### Check when completed

Agility Warm-up   _____
*high knees, shuffle, carioca, backpedal, butt kicks, power skips, spring

Dynamic Flexibility   _____
*tin man, walking hamstring, knee tuck/quad pull, front lunges, back lunges, spiderman

Kicking Without the Ball Drills   ### Check when completed

Quick Feet Full Approach Swings   1 x 5 swings   _____

One-Step Swings   1 x 5 swings   _____

No-Step Swings   1 x 5 swings   _____

Kicking With the Ball Drills   ### Check when completed

At-the-Upright Drill (no step)   5 kicks   _____

Over-the-Upright Drill)one step)   5 kicks   _____

Down-the-Sideline Right sideline (full approach) 5 kicks   _____

30 yard field goals middle   10 kicks   _____

Running Workout   ### Time of Run

3 x 440 yard run   1 minute 30 seconds for each run
                                                 3 minutes rest in between each run

Run 1: 440 yards   _____

Run 2: 440 yards   _____

Run 3: 440 yards   _____

Notes
1) Use a weight you can complete all the repetitions comfortably meaning you could do one or two more at the end of the set.
2) When you could do more than two more repetitions on a set move the weight used up 5 pounds.
3) Rest only 1 minute between sets and no longer.

Kicker Workout Recording Sheet

Wednesday
January Week 2

Flexibility   Check when completed

Agility Warm-up   _____
*high knees, shuffle, carioca, backpedal, butt kicks, power skips, spring

Dynamic Flexibility   _____
*tin man, walking hamstring, knee tuck/quad pull, front lunges, back lunges, spiderman

Kicking Without the Ball Drills   Check when completed

Quick Feet Full Approach Swings	1 x 10 swings	_____
One-Step Swings	1 x 10 swings	_____
No-Step Swings	1 x 10 swings	_____

Core Lifts   Weight Used

Power Cleans	3 x 8 reps	_____
Deadlift	3 x 8 reps	_____

Auxiliary Lifts   Weight Used

Glute Ham Raise	2 x 8 reps	_____
Push Press	2 x 8 reps	_____
Dips	2 x 8 reps	_____

Notes
1) Use a weight you can complete all the repetitions comfortably meaning you could do one or two more at the end of the set.
2) When you could do more than two more repetitions on a set move the weight used up 5 pounds.
3) Rest only 1 minute between sets and no longer.

Kicker Workout Recording Sheet

Thursday
January Week 2

Flexibility   Check when completed

Agility Warm-up   _____
*high knees, shuffle, carioca, backpedal, butt kicks, power skips, spring

Dynamic Flexibility   _____
*tin man, walking hamstring, knee tuck/quad pull, front lunges, back lunges, spiderman

Kicking Without the Ball Drills   Check when completed

Quick Feet Full Approach Swings   1 x 5 swings   _____

One-Step Swings   1 x 5 swings   _____

No-Step Swings   1 x 5 swings   _____

Kicking With the Ball Drills   Check when completed

At-the-Upright Drill (no step)   5 kicks   _____

Over-the-Upright Drill)one step)   5 kicks   _____

Down-the-Sideline Right sideline (full approach) 5 kicks   _____

30 yard field goals middle   10 kicks   _____

Running Workout   Time of Run

3 x 440 yard run   1 minute 30 seconds for each run
                                         3 minutes rest in between each run

Run 1: 440 yards   _____

Run 2: 440 yards   _____

Run 3: 440 yards   _____

Notes
1))Use a weight you can complete all the repetitions comfortably meaning you could do one or two more at the end of the set.
2) When you could do more than two more repetitions on a set move the weight used up 5 pounds.
3) Rest only 1 minute between sets and no longer.

Kicker Workout Recording Sheet

Friday
January Week 2

Flexibility   ## Check when completed

Agility Warm-up   _____
*high knees, shuffle, carioca, backpedal, butt kicks, power skips, spring

Dynamic Flexibility   _____
*tin man, walking hamstring, knee tuck/quad pull, front lunges, back lunges, spiderman

Kicking Without the Ball Drills   ## Check when completed

Quick Feet Full Approach Swings	1 x 10 swings	_____
One-Step Swings	1 x 10 swings	_____
No-Step Swings	1 x 10 swings	_____

Core Lifts   ## Weight Used

Lunges	3 x 8 reps	_____
Bench Press	3 x 8 reps	_____

Auxiliary Lifts   ## Weight Used

Lat Pulls	2 x 8 reps	_____
Leg Extension	2 x 8 reps	_____
Leg Curls	· 2 x 8 reps	_____
Neck	2 x 8 reps	_____
Arm Curls	2 x 8 reps	_____
Triceps Extensions	2 x 8 reps	_____

Notes
1) Use a weight you can complete all the repetitions comfortably meaning you could do one or two more at the end of the set.
2) When you could do more than two more repetitions on a set move the weight used up 5 pounds.
3) Rest only 1 minute between sets and no longer

Kicker Workout Recording Sheet

Monday
January Week 3

Flexibility   Check when completed

Agility Warm-up   _____
*high knees, shuffle, carioca, backpedal, butt kicks, power skips, spring

Dynamic Flexibility   _____
*tin man, walking hamstring, knee tuck/quad pull, front lunges, back lunges, spiderman

Kicking Without the Ball Drills   Check when completed

Quick Feet Full Approach Swings	1 x 10 swings	_____
One-Step Swings	1 x 10 swings	_____
No-Step Swings	1 x 10 swings	_____

Core Lifts   Weight Used

Squats	3 x 8 reps	_____
Close Grip Bench Press	3 x 8 reps	_____

Auxiliary Lifts   Weight Used

Lat Pulls	2 x 8 reps	_____
Front Raises (shoulders)	2 x 8 reps	_____
Lateral Raises (shoulders)	2 x 8 reps	_____
Arm Curls	2 x 8 reps	_____
Triceps Extensions	2 x 8 reps	_____

Notes
1) Use a weight you can complete all the repetitions comfortably meaning you could do one or two more at the end of the set.
2) When you could do more than two more repetitions on a set move the weight used up 5 pounds.
3) Rest only 1 minute between sets and no longer.

Kicker Workout Recording Sheet

Tuesday
January Week 3

Flexibility   Check when completed

Agility Warm-up   _____
*high knees, shuffle, carioca, backpedal, butt kicks, power skips, spring

Dynamic Flexibility   _____
*tin man, walking hamstring, knee tuck/quad pull, front lunges, back lunges, spiderman

Kicking Without the Ball Drills   Check when completed

Quick Feet Full Approach Swings   1 x 5 swings   _____

One-Step Swings   1 x 5 swings   _____

No-Step Swings   1 x 5 swings   _____

Kicking With the Ball Drills   Check when completed

At-the-Upright Drill (no step)   5 kicks   _____

Over-the-Upright Drill)one step)   5 kicks   _____

Down-the-Sideline Right sideline (full approach) 5 kicks   _____

30 yard field goals middle   10 kicks   _____

Running Workout   ## Time of Run

3 x 440 yard run   1 minute 30 seconds for each run
                                                 3 minutes rest in between each run

Run 1: 440 yards   _____

Run 2: 440 yards   _____

Run 3: 440 yards   _____

Notes
1) Use a weight you can complete all the repetitions comfortably meaning you could do one or two more at the end of the set.
2) When you could do more than two more repetitions on a set move the weight used up 5 pounds.
3) Rest only 1 minute between sets and no longer.

Kicker Workout Recording Sheet

Wednesday
January Week 3

Flexibility   Check when completed

Agility Warm-up   _____
*high knees, shuffle, carioca, backpedal, butt kicks, power skips, spring

Dynamic Flexibility   _____
*tin man, walking hamstring, knee tuck/quad pull, front lunges, back lunges, spiderman

Kicking Without the Ball Drills   Check when completed

Quick Feet Full Approach Swings   1 x 10 swings   _____

One-Step Swings   1 x 10 swings   _____

No-Step Swings   1 x 10 swings   _____

Core Lifts   Weight Used

Power Cleans   3 x 8 reps   _____

Deadlift   3 x 8 reps   _____

Auxiliary Lifts   Weight Used

Glute Ham Raise   2 x 8 reps   _____

Push Press   2 x 8 reps   _____

Dips   2 x 8 reps   _____

Notes
1) Use a weight you can complete all the repetitions comfortably meaning you could do one or two more at the end of the set.
2) When you could do more than two more repetitions on a set move the weight used up 5 pounds.
3) Rest only 1 minute between sets and no longer.

Kicker Workout Recording Sheet

Thursday
January Week 3

Flexibility   ## Check when completed

Agility Warm-up   _____
*high knees, shuffle, carioca, backpedal, butt kicks, power skips, spring

Dynamic Flexibility   _____
*tin man, walking hamstring, knee tuck/quad pull, front lunges, back lunges, spiderman

Kicking Without the Ball Drills   ## Check when completed

Quick Feet Full Approach Swings   1 x 5 swings   _____

One-Step Swings   1 x 5 swings   _____

No-Step Swings   1 x 5 swings   _____

Kicking With the Ball Drills   ## Check when completed

At-the-Upright Drill (no step)   5 kicks   _____

Over-the-Upright Drill)one step)   5 kicks   _____

Down-the-Sideline Right sideline (full approach) 5 kicks   _____

30 yard field goals middle   10 kicks   _____

Running Workout   ## Time of Run

3 x 440 yard run   1 minute 30 seconds for each run
                                                 3 minutes rest in between each run

Run 1: 440 yards   _____

Run 2: 440 yards   _____

Run 3: 440 yards   _____

Notes
   1) Use a weight you can complete all the repetitions comfortably meaning you could
      do one or two more at the end of the set.
   2) When you could do more than two more repetitions on a set move the weight used up 5 pounds.
   3) Rest only 1 minute between sets and no longer.

Kicker Workout Recording Sheet

Friday
January Week 3

Flexibility   ### Check when completed

Agility Warm-up   _____
*high knees, shuffle, carioca, backpedal, butt kicks, power skips, spring

Dynamic Flexibility   _____
*tin man, walking hamstring, knee tuck/quad pull, front lunges, back lunges, spiderman

Kicking Without the Ball Drills   ### Check when completed

Quick Feet Full Approach Swings   1 x 10 swings   _____

One-Step Swings   1 x 10 swings   _____

No-Step Swings   1 x 10 swings   _____

Core Lifts   ### Weight Used

Lunges   3 x 8 reps   _____

Bench Press   3 x 8 reps   _____

Auxiliary Lifts   ### Weight Used

Lat Pulls   2 x 8 reps   _____

Leg Extension   2 x 8 reps   _____

Leg Curls   2 x 8 reps   _____

Neck   2 x 8 reps   _____

Arm Curls   2 x 8 reps   _____

Triceps Extensions   2 x 8 reps   _____

Notes
1) Use a weight you can complete all the repetitions comfortably meaning you could do one or two more at the end of the set.
2) When you could do more than two more repetitions on a set move the weight used up 5 pounds.
3) Rest only 1 minute between sets and no longer

Kicker Workout Recording Sheet

Monday
January Week 4

Flexibility   Check when completed

Agility Warm-up   _____
*high knees, shuffle, carioca, backpedal, butt kicks, power skips, spring

Dynamic Flexibility   _____
*tin man, walking hamstring, knee tuck/quad pull, front lunges, back lunges, spiderman

Kicking Without the Ball Drills   Check when completed

Quick Feet Full Approach Swings	1 x 10 swings	_____
One-Step Swings	1 x 10 swings	_____
No-Step Swings	1 x 10 swings	_____

Core Lifts   Weight Used

Squats	3 x 8 reps	_____
Close Grip Bench Press	3 x 8 reps	_____

Auxiliary Lifts   Weight Used

Lat Pulls	2 x 8 reps	_____
Front Raises (shoulders)	2 x 8 reps	_____
Lateral Raises (shoulders)	2 x 8 reps	_____
Arm Curls	2 x 8 reps	_____
Triceps Extensions	2 x 8 reps	_____

Notes
1) Use a weight you can complete all the repetitions comfortably meaning you could do one or two more at the end of the set.
2) When you could do more than two more repetitions on a set move the weight used up 5 pounds.
3) Rest only 1 minute between sets and no longer.

Kicker Workout Recording Sheet

Tuesday
January Week 4

Flexibility

Check when completed

Agility Warm-up   _____
*high knees, shuffle, carioca, backpedal, butt kicks, power skips, spring

Dynamic Flexibility   _____
*tin man, walking hamstring, knee tuck/quad pull, front lunges, back lunges, spiderman

Kicking Without the Ball Drills

Check when completed

Quick Feet Full Approach Swings   1 x 5 swings   _____

One-Step Swings   1 x 5 swings   _____

No-Step Swings   1 x 5 swings   _____

Kicking With the Ball Drills

Check when completed

At-the-Upright Drill (no step)   5 kicks   _____

Over-the-Upright Drill)one step)   5 kicks   _____

Down-the-Sideline Right sideline (full approach) 5 kicks _____

30 yard field goals middle   10 kicks   _____

Running Workout

Time of Run

3 x 440 yard run   1 minute 30 seconds for each run
                                     3 minutes rest in between each run

Run 1: 440 yards   _____

Run 2: 440 yards   _____

Run 3: 440 yards   _____

Notes
1) Use a weight you can complete all the repetitions comfortably meaning you could do one or two more at the end of the set.
2) When you could do more than two more repetitions on a set move the weight used up 5 pounds.
3) Rest only 1 minute between sets and no longer.

Kicker Workout Recording Sheet

Wednesday
January Week 4

Flexibility   ### Check when completed

Agility Warm-up   _____
*high knees, shuffle, carioca, backpedal, butt kicks, power skips, spring

Dynamic Flexibility   _____
*tin man, walking hamstring, knee tuck/quad pull, front lunges, back lunges, spiderman

Kicking Without the Ball Drills   ### Check when completed

Quick Feet Full Approach Swings   1 x 10 swings   _____

One-Step Swings   1 x 10 swings   _____

No-Step Swings   1 x 10 swings   _____

Core Lifts   ### Weight Used

Power Cleans   3 x 8 reps   _____

Deadlift   3 x 8 reps   _____

Auxiliary Lifts   ### Weight Used

Glute Ham Raise   2 x 8 reps   _____

Push Press   2 x 8 reps   _____

Dips   2 x 8 reps   _____

Notes
   1) Use a weight you can complete all the repetitions comfortably meaning you could do one
      or two more at the end of the set.
   2) When you could do more than two more repetitions on a set move the weight used up 5 pounds.
   3) Rest only 1 minute between sets and no longer.

Kicker Workout Recording Sheet

Thursday
January Week 4

Flexibility	Check when completed

Agility Warm-up   _____
*high knees, shuffle, carioca, backpedal, butt kicks, power skips, spring

Dynamic Flexibility   _____
*tin man, walking hamstring, knee tuck/quad pull, front lunges, back lunges, spiderman

Kicking Without the Ball Drills   Check when completed

Quick Feet Full Approach Swings	1 x 5 swings	_____
One-Step Swings	1 x 5 swings	_____
No-Step Swings	1 x 5 swings	_____

Kicking With the Ball Drills   Check when completed

At-the-Upright Drill (no step)	5 kicks	_____
Over-the-Upright Drill)one step)	5 kicks	_____
Down-the-Sideline Right sideline (full approach)	5 kicks	_____
30 yard field goals middle	10 kicks	_____

Running Workout   Time of Run

3 x 440 yard run

1 minute 30 seconds for each run
3 minutes rest in between each run

Run 1: 440 yards	_____
Run 2: 440 yards	_____
Run 3: 440 yards	_____

Notes
1) Use a weight you can complete all the repetitions comfortably meaning you could do one or two more at the end of the set.
2) When you could do more than two more repetitions on a set move the weight used up 5 pounds.
3) Rest only 1 minute between sets and no longer.

Kicker Workout Recording Sheet

Friday
January Week 4

Flexibility   Check when completed

Agility Warm-up   _____
*high knees, shuffle, carioca, backpedal, butt kicks, power skips, spring

Dynamic Flexibility   _____
*tin man, walking hamstring, knee tuck/quad pull, front lunges, back lunges, spiderman

Kicking Without the Ball Drills   Check when completed

Quick Feet Full Approach Swings   1 x 10 swings   _____

One-Step Swings   1 x 10 swings   _____

No-Step Swings   1 x 10 swings   _____

Core Lifts   Weight Used

Lunges   3 x 8 reps   _____

Bench Press   3 x 8 reps   _____

Auxiliary Lifts   Weight Used

Lat Pulls   2 x 8 reps   _____

Leg Extension   2 x 8 reps   _____

Leg Curls   2 x 8 reps   _____

Neck   2 x 8 reps   _____

Arm Curls   2 x 8 reps   _____

Triceps Extensions   2 x 8 reps   _____

Notes
1) Use a weight you can complete all the repetitions comfortably meaning you could do one or two more at the end of the set.
2) When you could do more than two more repetitions on a set move the weight used up 5 pounds.
3) Rest only 1 minute between sets and no longer

February

Workout Charts

High School KICKERS
OFF-SEASON Training Calendar
February

SUNDAY	MONDAY	TUESDAY	WEDNESDAY	THURSDAY	FRIDAY	SATURDAY
Week 1 NO WORKOUT REST	Week 1 **Kickers** Quick Feet Drills Weightlifting	Week 1 **Kick** 25 reps into net Ball Contact Kicking Workout Running Workout	Week 1 **Kickers** Quick Feet Drills Weightlifting	Week 1 **Kick** 25 reps into net Ball Contact Kicking Workout Running Workout	Week 1 **Kickers** Quick Feet Drills Weightlifting	Week 1 No training prescribed rest or participate in light physical activity. <u>i.e.</u> basketball, biking, etc.
Week 2 NO WORKOUT REST	Week 2 **Kickers** Quick Feet Drills Weightlifting	Week 2 **Kick** 25 reps into net Ball Contact Kicking Workout Running Workout	Week 2 **Kickers** Quick Feet Drills Weightlifting	Week 2 **Kick** 25 reps into net Ball Contact Kicking Workout Running Workout	Week 2 **Kickers** Quick Feet Drills Weightlifting	Week 2 No training prescribed rest or participate in light physical activity. <u>i.e.</u> basketball, biking, etc.
Week 3 NO WORKOUT REST	Week 3 **Kickers** Quick Feet Drills Weightlifting	Week 3 **Kick** 25 reps into net Ball Contact Kicking Workout Running Workout	Week 3 **Kickers** Quick Feet Drills Weightlifting	Week 3 **Kick** 25 reps into net Ball Contact Kicking Workout Running Workout	Week 3 **Kickers** Quick Feet Drills Weightlifting	Week 3 No training prescribed rest or participate in light physical activity. <u>i.e.</u> basketball, biking, etc.
Week 4 NO WORKOUT REST	Week 4 **Kickers** Quick Feet Drills Weightlifting	Week 4 **Kick** 25 reps into net Ball Contact Kicking Workout Running Workout	Week 4 **Kickers** Quick Feet Drills Weightlifting	Week 4 **Kick** 25 reps into net Ball Contact Kicking Workout Running Workout	Week 4 **Kickers** Quick Feet Drills Weightlifting	Week 4 No training prescribed rest or participate in light physical activity. <u>i.e.</u> basketball, biking, etc.

High School KICKERS
OFF-SEASON SPEED and STRENGTH Training Program
February

MONDAY	TUESDAY	WEDNESDAY	THURSDAY	FRIDAY
Flexibility Agility Warm-up Dynamic Flexibility ------------------	**Flexibility** Agility Warm-up Dynamic Flexibility ------------------	**Flexibility** Agility Warm-up Dynamic Flexibility ------------------	**Flexibility** Agility Warm-up Dynamic Flexibility ------------------	**Flexibility** Agility Warm-up Dynamic Flexibility ------------------
Kicker Drills **1 set of 10** No Step Drill One Step Drill Quick Feet Full Approach Drill ------------------	**Kicker Drills** **1 set of 5** No Step Drill One Step Drill Quick Feet Full Approach Drill	**Kicker Drills** **1 set of 10** No Step Drill One Step Drill Quick Feet Full Approach Drill ------------------	**Kicker Drills** **1 set of 5** No Step Drill One Step Drill Quick Feet Full Approach Drill	**Kicker Drills** **1 set of 10** No Step Drill One Step Drill Quick Feet Full Approach Drill ------------------
Core Lifts **3 sets of 5** Squat Close Grip Bench Press ------------------	**Kicking Workout** 25 Kicks into the NET ------------------ **Running Workout** 10 x 40 yd sprints – ¾ speed 45 sec. rest between each	**Core Lifts** **3 sets of 5** Cleans Deadlift ------------------ **Auxiliary Lifts** **2 sets of 8** Glute Ham Raise Push Press Dips	**Kicking Workout** 25 Kicks into the NET ------------------ **Running Workout** 10 x 40 yd sprints – ¾ speed 45 sec. rest between each	**Core Lifts** **3 sets of 5** Lunges Bench Press ------------------
Auxiliary Lifts **2 sets of 8** Lat Pull Front Raises Lateral Raises Arm Curls Tricep Extension				**Auxiliary Lifts** **2 sets of 8** Lat Pulls Leg Extension Leg Curls Neck Arm Curls Tricep Extension

Agility Warm-up Routine
*15 yards – down and back using each movement
High knees
Shuffle
Carioca
Backpedal
Butt kicks
Power skips
Sprint

Dynamic Flexibility Routine
*10 yards – down and back using each movement
Tin soldiers
Walking Hamstring
Knee Tuck/Quad Pull
Front Lunges
Back Lunges
Spiderman

Kicker Workout Recording Sheet

Monday
February Week 1

Flexibility   Check when completed

Agility Warm-up   _____
*high knees, shuffle, carioca, backpedal, butt kicks, power skips, spring

Dynamic Flexibility   _____
*tin man, walking hamstring, knee tuck/quad pull, front lunges, back lunges, spiderman

Kicking Without the Ball Drills   Check when completed

Quick Feet Full Approach Swings   1 x 10 swings   _____

One-Step Swings   1 x 10 swings   _____

No-Step Swings   1 x 10 swings   _____

Core Lifts   Weight Used

Squats   3 x 5 reps   _____

Close Grip Bench Press   3 x 5 reps   _____

Auxiliary Lifts   Weight Used

Lat Pulls   2 x 8 reps   _____

Front Raises (shoulders)   2 x 8 reps   _____

Lateral Raises (shoulders)   2 x 8 reps   _____

Arm Curls   2 x 8 reps   _____

Triceps Extensions   2 x 8 reps   _____

Notes
1) Use a weight you can complete all the repetitions comfortably meaning you could do one or two more at the end of the set.
2) When you could do more than two more repetitions on a set move the weight used up 5 pounds.
3) Rest only 1 minute between sets and no longer.

Kicker Workout Recording Sheet

Tuesday
February Week 1

Flexibility   ### Check when completed

Agility Warm-up   _____
*high knees, shuffle, carioca, backpedal, butt kicks, power skips, spring

Dynamic Flexibility   _____
*tin man, walking hamstring, knee tuck/quad pull, front lunges, back lunges, spiderman

Kicking Without the Ball Drills   ### Check when completed

Quick Feet Full Approach Swings   1 x 5 swings   _____

One-Step Swings   1 x 5 swings   _____

No-Step Swings   1 x 5 swings   _____

Kicking With the Ball Drills   ### Check when completed

At-the-Upright Drill (no step)   5 kicks   _____

Over-the-Upright Drill)one step)   5 kicks   _____

Down-the-Sideline Right sideline (full approach) 5 kicks   _____

30 yard field goals middle   10 kicks   _____

Running Workout   ### Time of Run

10 x 40 yard dashes   run ¾ speed for each rep
                                         45 seconds rest in between each run

Notes
1) Use a weight you can complete all the repetitions comfortably meaning you could do one or two more at the end of the set.
2) When you could do more than two more repetitions on a set move the weight used up 5 pounds.
3) Rest only 1 minute between sets and no longer.

Kicker Workout Recording Sheet

Wednesday
February Week 1

Flexibility   Check when completed

Agility Warm-up   _____
*high knees, shuffle, carioca, backpedal, butt kicks, power skips, spring

Dynamic Flexibility   _____
*tin man, walking hamstring, knee tuck/quad pull, front lunges, back lunges, spiderman

Kicking Without the Ball Drills   Check when completed

Quick Feet Full Approach Swings   1 x 10 swings   _____

One-Step Swings   1 x 10 swings   _____

No-Step Swings   1 x 10 swings   _____

Core Lifts   Weight Used

Power Cleans   3 x 5 reps   _____

Deadlift   3 x 5 reps   _____

Auxiliary Lifts   Weight Used

Glute Ham Raise   2 x 8 reps   _____

Push Press   2 x 8 reps   _____

Dips   2 x 8 reps   _____

Notes
1) Use a weight you can complete all the repetitions comfortably meaning you could do one or two more at the end of the set.
2) When you could do more than two more repetitions on a set move the weight used up 5 pounds.
3) Rest only 1 minute between sets and no longer.

Kicker Workout Recording Sheet

Thursday
February Week 1

Flexibility	Check when completed

Agility Warm-up   _____
*high knees, shuffle, carioca, backpedal, butt kicks, power skips, spring

Dynamic Flexibility   _____
*tin man, walking hamstring, knee tuck/quad pull, front lunges, back lunges, spiderman

Kicking Without the Ball Drills   Check when completed

Quick Feet Full Approach Swings	1 x 5 swings	_____
One-Step Swings	1 x 5 swings	_____
No-Step Swings	1 x 5 swings	_____

Kicking With the Ball Drills   Check when completed

At-the-Upright Drill (no step)	5 kicks	_____
Over-the-Upright Drill)one step)	5 kicks	_____
Down-the-Sideline Right sideline (full approach) 5 kicks		_____
30 yard field goals middle	10 kicks	_____

Running Workout   Time of Run

10 x 40 yard dashes

run ¾ speed for each rep
45 seconds rest in between each run

Notes
1) Use a weight you can complete all the repetitions comfortably meaning you could do one or two more at the end of the set.
2) When you could do more than two more repetitions on a set move the weight used up 5 pounds.
3) Rest only 1 minute between sets and no longer.

Kicker Workout Recording Sheet

Friday
February Week 1

Flexibility   Check when completed

Agility Warm-up   _____
*high knees, shuffle, carioca, backpedal, butt kicks, power skips, spring

Dynamic Flexibility   _____
*tin man, walking hamstring, knee tuck/quad pull, front lunges, back lunges, spiderman

Kicking Without the Ball Drills   Check when completed

Quick Feet Full Approach Swings	1 x 10 swings	_____
One-Step Swings	1 x 10 swings	_____
No-Step Swings	1 x 10 swings	_____

Core Lifts   Weight Used

Lunges	3 x 5 reps	_____
Bench Press	3 x 5 reps	_____

Auxiliary Lifts   Weight Used

Lat Pulls	2 x 8 reps	_____
Leg Extension	2 x 8 reps	_____
Leg Curls	2 x 8 reps	_____
Neck	2 x 8 reps	_____
Arm Curls	2 x 8 reps	_____
Triceps Extensions	2 x 8 reps	_____

Notes
1) Use a weight you can complete all the repetitions comfortably meaning you could do one or two more at the end of the set.
2) When you could do more than two more repetitions on a set move the weight used up 5 pounds.
3) Rest only 1 minute between sets and no longer

Kicker Workout Recording Sheet

Monday
February Week 2

Flexibility   Check when completed

Agility Warm-up   _____
*high knees, shuffle, carioca, backpedal, butt kicks, power skips, spring

Dynamic Flexibility   _____
*tin man, walking hamstring, knee tuck/quad pull, front lunges, back lunges, spiderman

Kicking Without the Ball Drills   Check when completed

Quick Feet Full Approach Swings   1 x 10 swings   _____

One-Step Swings   1 x 10 swings   _____

No-Step Swings   1 x 10 swings   _____

Core Lifts   Weight Used

Squats   3 x 5 reps   _____

Close Grip Bench Press   3 x 5 reps   _____

Auxiliary Lifts   Weight Used

Lat Pulls   2 x 8 reps   _____

Front Raises (shoulders)   2 x 8 reps   _____

Lateral Raises (shoulders)   2 x 8 reps   _____

Arm Curls   2 x 8 reps   _____

Triceps Extensions   2 x 8 reps   _____

Notes
1) Use a weight you can complete all the repetitions comfortably meaning you could do one or two more at the end of the set.
2) When you could do more than two more repetitions on a set move the weight used up 5 pounds.
3) Rest only 1 minute between sets and no longer.

Kicker Workout Recording Sheet

Tuesday
February Week 2

Flexibility   Check when completed

Agility Warm-up   _____
*high knees, shuffle, carioca, backpedal, butt kicks, power skips, spring

Dynamic Flexibility   _____
*tin man, walking hamstring, knee tuck/quad pull, front lunges, back lunges, spiderman

Kicking Without the Ball Drills   Check when completed

Quick Feet Full Approach Swings   1 x 5 swings   _____

One-Step Swings   1 x 5 swings   _____

No-Step Swings   1 x 5 swings   _____

Kicking With the Ball Drills   Check when completed

At-the-Upright Drill (no step)   5 kicks   _____

Over-the-Upright Drill)one step) 5 kicks   _____

Down-the-Sideline Right sideline (full approach) 5 kicks _____

30 yard field goals middle   10 kicks   _____

Running Workout   Time of Run

10 x 40 yard dashes   run ¾ speed for each rep
                                   45 seconds rest in between each run

Notes
1) Use a weight you can complete all the repetitions comfortably meaning you could do one or two more at the end of the set.
2) When you could do more than two more repetitions on a set move the weight used up 5 pounds.
3) Rest only 1 minute between sets and no longer.

Kicker Workout Recording Sheet

Wednesday
February Week 2

Flexibility   Check when completed

Agility Warm-up   _____
*high knees, shuffle, carioca, backpedal, butt kicks, power skips, spring

Dynamic Flexibility   _____
*tin man, walking hamstring, knee tuck/quad pull, front lunges, back lunges, spiderman

Kicking Without the Ball Drills   Check when completed

Quick Feet Full Approach Swings   1 x 10 swings   _____

One-Step Swings   1 x 10 swings   _____

No-Step Swings   1 x 10 swings   _____

Core Lifts   Weight Used

Power Cleans   3 x 5 reps   _____

Deadlift   3 x 5 reps   _____

Auxiliary Lifts   Weight Used

Glute Ham Raise   2 x 8 reps   _____

Push Press   2 x 8 reps   _____

Dips   2 x 8 reps   _____

Notes
1) Use a weight you can complete all the repetitions comfortably meaning you could do one or two more at the end of the set.
2) When you could do more than two more repetitions on a set move the weight used up 5 pounds.
3) Rest only 1 minute between sets and no longer.

Kicker Workout Recording Sheet

Thursday
February Week 2

Flexibility   ## Check when completed

Agility Warm-up   _____
*high knees, shuffle, carioca, backpedal, butt kicks, power skips, spring

Dynamic Flexibility   _____
*tin man, walking hamstring, knee tuck/quad pull, front lunges, back lunges, spiderman

Kicking Without the Ball Drills   ## Check when completed

Quick Feet Full Approach Swings   1 x 5 swings   _____

One-Step Swings   1 x 5 swings   _____

No-Step Swings   1 x 5 swings   _____

Kicking With the Ball Drills   ## Check when completed

At-the-Upright Drill (no step)   5 kicks   _____

Over-the-Upright Drill)one step)   5 kicks   _____

Down-the-Sideline Right sideline (full approach) 5 kicks   _____

30 yard field goals middle   10 kicks   _____

Running Workout   ## Time of Run

10 x 40 yard dashes   run ¾ speed for each rep
                                         45 seconds rest in between each run

Notes
1) Use a weight you can complete all the repetitions comfortably meaning you could
   do one or two more at the end of the set.
2) When you could do more than two more repetitions on a set move the weight used up 5 pounds.
3) Rest only 1 minute between sets and no longer.

Kicker Workout Recording Sheet

Friday
February Week 2

Flexibility   Check when completed

Agility Warm-up   _____
*high knees, shuffle, carioca, backpedal, butt kicks, power skips, spring

Dynamic Flexibility   _____
*tin man, walking hamstring, knee tuck/quad pull, front lunges, back lunges, spiderman

Kicking Without the Ball Drills   Check when completed

Quick Feet Full Approach Swings	1 x 10 swings	_____
One-Step Swings	1 x 10 swings	_____
No-Step Swings	1 x 10 swings	_____

Core Lifts   Weight Used

| Lunges | 3 x 5 reps | _____ |
| Bench Press | 3 x 5 reps | _____ |

Auxiliary Lifts   Weight Used

Lat Pulls	2 x 8 reps	_____
Leg Extension	2 x 8 reps	_____
Leg Curls	2 x 8 reps	_____
Neck	2 x 8 reps	_____
Arm Curls	2 x 8 reps	_____
Triceps Extensions	2 x 8 reps	_____

Notes
1) Use a weight you can complete all the repetitions comfortably meaning you could do one or two more at the end of the set.
2) When you could do more than two more repetitions on a set move the weight used up 5 pounds.
3) Rest only 1 minute between sets and no longer

Kicker Workout Recording Sheet

Monday
February Week 3

Flexibility

Check when completed

Agility Warm-up   _____
*high knees, shuffle, carioca, backpedal, butt kicks, power skips, spring

Dynamic Flexibility   _____
*tin man, walking hamstring, knee tuck/quad pull, front lunges, back lunges, spiderman

Kicking Without the Ball Drills

Check when completed

Quick Feet Full Approach Swings	1 x 10 swings	_____
One-Step Swings	1 x 10 swings	_____
No-Step Swings	1 x 10 swings	_____

Core Lifts

Weight Used

Squats	3 x 5 reps	_____
Close Grip Bench Press	3 x 5 reps	_____

Auxiliary Lifts

Weight Used

Lat Pulls	2 x 8 reps	_____
Front Raises (shoulders)	2 x 8 reps	_____
Lateral Raises (shoulders)	2 x 8 reps	_____
Arm Curls	2 x 8 reps	_____
Triceps Extensions	2 x 8 reps	_____

Notes
1) Use a weight you can complete all the repetitions comfortably meaning you could do one or two more at the end of the set.
2) When you could do more than two more repetitions on a set move the weight used up 5 pounds.
3) Rest only 1 minute between sets and no longer.

Kicker Workout Recording Sheet

Tuesday
February Week 3

Flexibility   ### Check when completed

Agility Warm-up   _____
*high knees, shuffle, carioca, backpedal, butt kicks, power skips, spring

Dynamic Flexibility   _____
*tin man, walking hamstring, knee tuck/quad pull, front lunges, back lunges, spiderman

Kicking Without the Ball Drills   ### Check when completed

Quick Feet Full Approach Swings   1 x 5 swings   _____

One-Step Swings   1 x 5 swings   _____

No-Step Swings   1 x 5 swings   _____

Kicking With the Ball Drills   ### Check when completed

At-the-Upright Drill (no step)   5 kicks   _____

Over-the-Upright Drill)one step)   5 kicks   _____

Down-the-Sideline Right sideline (full approach) 5 kicks _____

30 yard field goals middle   10 kicks   _____

Running Workout   ### Time of Run

10 x 40 yard dashes   run ¾ speed for each rep
                                                  45 seconds rest in between each run

Notes
1) Use a weight you can complete all the repetitions comfortably meaning you could do one or two more at the end of the set.
2) When you could do more than two more repetitions on a set move the weight used up 5 pounds.
3) Rest only 1 minute between sets and no longer.

Kicker Workout Recording Sheet

Wednesday
February Week 3

Flexibility   Check when completed

Agility Warm-up   _____
*high knees, shuffle, carioca, backpedal, butt kicks, power skips, spring

Dynamic Flexibility   _____
*tin man, walking hamstring, knee tuck/quad pull, front lunges, back lunges, spiderman

Kicking Without the Ball Drills   Check when completed

Quick Feet Full Approach Swings	1 x 10 swings	_____
One-Step Swings	1 x 10 swings	_____
No-Step Swings	1 x 10 swings	_____

Core Lifts   Weight Used

Power Cleans	3 x 5 reps	_____
Deadlift	3 x 5 reps	_____

Auxiliary Lifts   Weight Used

Glute Ham Raise	2 x 8 reps	_____
Push Press	2 x 8 reps	_____
Dips	2 x 8 reps	_____

Notes
1) Use a weight you can complete all the repetitions comfortably meaning you could do one or two more at the end of the set.
2) When you could do more than two more repetitions on a set move the weight used up 5 pounds.
3) Rest only 1 minute between sets and no longer.

Kicker Workout Recording Sheet

Thursday
February Week 3

Flexibility   ### Check when completed

Agility Warm-up   _____
*high knees, shuffle, carioca, backpedal, butt kicks, power skips, spring

Dynamic Flexibility   _____
*tin man, walking hamstring, knee tuck/quad pull, front lunges, back lunges, spiderman

Kicking Without the Ball Drills   ### Check when completed

Quick Feet Full Approach Swings   1 x 5 swings   _____

One-Step Swings   1 x 5 swings   _____

No-Step Swings   1 x 5 swings   _____

Kicking With the Ball Drills   ### Check when completed

At-the-Upright Drill (no step)   5 kicks   _____

Over-the-Upright Drill)one step)   5 kicks   _____

Down-the-Sideline Right sideline (full approach) 5 kicks _____

30 yard field goals middle   10 kicks   _____

Running Workout   ### Time of Run

10 x 40 yard dashes   run ¾ speed for each rep
                                                         45 seconds rest in between each run

Notes
1) Use a weight you can complete all the repetitions comfortably meaning you could do one or two more at the end of the set.
2) When you could do more than two more repetitions on a set move the weight used up 5 pounds.
3) Rest only 1 minute between sets and no longer.

Kicker Workout Recording Sheet

Friday
February Week 3

Flexibility   Check when completed

Agility Warm-up   _____
*high knees, shuffle, carioca, backpedal, butt kicks, power skips, spring

Dynamic Flexibility   _____
*tin man, walking hamstring, knee tuck/quad pull, front lunges, back lunges, spiderman

Kicking Without the Ball Drills   Check when completed

Quick Feet Full Approach Swings   1 x 10 swings   _____

One-Step Swings   1 x 10 swings   _____

No-Step Swings   1 x 10 swings   _____

Core Lifts   Weight Used

Lunges   3 x 5 reps   _____

Bench Press   3 x 5 reps   _____

Auxiliary Lifts   Weight Used

Lat Pulls   2 x 8 reps   _____

Leg Extension   2 x 8 reps   _____

Leg Curls   2 x 8 reps   _____   .

Neck   2 x 8 reps   _____

Arm Curls   2 x 8 reps   _____

Triceps Extensions   2 x 8 reps   _____

Notes
1) Use a weight you can complete all the repetitions comfortably meaning you could do one or two more at the end of the set.
2) When you could do more than two more repetitions on a set move the weight used up 5 pounds.
3) Rest only 1 minute between sets and no longer.

Kicker Workout Recording Sheet

Monday
February Week 4

Flexibility   ### Check when completed

Agility Warm-up   _____
*high knees, shuffle, carioca, backpedal, butt kicks, power skips, spring

Dynamic Flexibility   _____
*tin man, walking hamstring, knee tuck/quad pull, front lunges, back lunges, spiderman

Kicking Without the Ball Drills   ### Check when completed

Quick Feet Full Approach Swings   1 x 10 swings   _____

One-Step Swings   1 x 10 swings   _____

No-Step Swings   1 x 10 swings   _____

Core Lifts   ### Weight Used

Squats   3 x 5 reps   _____

Close Grip Bench Press   3 x 5 reps   _____

Auxiliary Lifts   ### Weight Used

Lat Pulls   2 x 8 reps   _____

Front Raises (shoulders)   2 x 8 reps   _____

Lateral Raises (shoulders)   2 x 8 reps   _____

Arm Curls   2 x 8 reps   _____

Triceps Extensions   2 x 8 reps   _____

Notes
1) Use a weight you can complete all the repetitions comfortably meaning you could do one or two more at the end of the set.
2) When you could do more than two more repetitions on a set move the weight used up 5 pounds.
3) Rest only 1 minute between sets and no longer.

Kicker Workout Recording Sheet

Tuesday
February Week 4

Flexibility   ## Check when completed

Agility Warm-up   _____
*high knees, shuffle, carioca, backpedal, butt kicks, power skips, spring

Dynamic Flexibility   _____
*tin man, walking hamstring, knee tuck/quad pull, front lunges, back lunges, spiderman

Kicking Without the Ball Drills   ## Check when completed

Quick Feet Full Approach Swings   1 x 5 swings   _____

One-Step Swings   1 x 5 swings   _____

No-Step Swings   1 x 5 swings   _____

Kicking With the Ball Drills   ## Check when completed

At-the-Upright Drill (no step)   5 kicks   _____

Over-the-Upright Drill)one step)   5 kicks   _____

Down-the-Sideline Right sideline (full approach) 5 kicks _____

30 yard field goals middle   10 kicks   _____

Running Workout   ## Time of Run

10 x 40 yard dashes   run ¾ speed for each rep
                                                 45 seconds rest in between each run

Notes
1) Use a weight you can complete all the repetitions comfortably meaning you could do one or two more at the end of the set.
2) When you could do more than two more repetitions on a set move the weight used up 5 pounds.
3) Rest only 1 minute between sets and no longer.

Kicker Workout Recording Sheet

Wednesday
February Week 4

Flexibility   ### Check when completed

Agility Warm-up   _____
*high knees, shuffle, carioca, backpedal, butt kicks, power skips, spring

Dynamic Flexibility   _____
*tin man, walking hamstring, knee tuck/quad pull, front lunges, back lunges, spiderman

Kicking Without the Ball Drills   ### Check when completed

Quick Feet Full Approach Swings	1 x 10 swings	_____
One-Step Swings	1 x 10 swings	_____
No-Step Swings	1 x 10 swings	_____

Core Lifts   ### Weight Used

Power Cleans	3 x 5 reps	_____
Deadlift	3 x 5 reps	_____

Auxiliary Lifts   ### Weight Used

Glute Ham Raise	2 x 8 reps	_____
Push Press	2 x 8 reps	_____
Dips	2 x 8 reps	_____

Notes
1) Use a weight you can complete all the repetitions comfortably meaning you could do one or two more at the end of the set.
2) When you could do more than two more repetitions on a set move the weight used up 5 pounds.
3) Rest only 1 minute between sets and no longer.

Kicker Workout Recording Sheet

Thursday
February Week 4

Flexibility   ## Check when completed

Agility Warm-up   _____
*high knees, shuffle, carioca, backpedal, butt kicks, power skips, spring

Dynamic Flexibility   _____
*tin man, walking hamstring, knee tuck/quad pull, front lunges, back lunges, spiderman

Kicking Without the Ball Drills   ## Check when completed

Quick Feet Full Approach Swings   1 x 5 swings   _____

One-Step Swings   1 x 5 swings   _____

No-Step Swings   1 x 5 swings   _____

Kicking With the Ball Drills   ## Check when completed

At-the-Upright Drill (no step)   5 kicks   _____

Over-the-Upright Drill)one step)   5 kicks   _____

Down-the-Sideline Right sideline (full approach) 5 kicks   _____

30 yard field goals middle   10 kicks   _____

Running Workout   ## Time of Run

10 x 40 yard dashes   run ¾ speed for each rep
                                             45 seconds rest in between each run

Notes
1) Use a weight you can complete all the repetitions comfortably meaning you could
   do one or two more at the end of the set.
2) When you could do more than two more repetitions on a set move the weight used up 5 pounds.
3) Rest only 1 minute between sets and no longer.

Kicker Workout Recording Sheet

Friday
February Week 4

Flexibility   Check when completed

Agility Warm-up   _____
*high knees, shuffle, carioca, backpedal, butt kicks, power skips, spring

Dynamic Flexibility   _____
*tin man, walking hamstring, knee tuck/quad pull, front lunges, back lunges, spiderman

Kicking Without the Ball Drills   Check when completed

Quick Feet Full Approach Swings   1 x 10 swings   _____

One-Step Swings   1 x 10 swings   _____

No-Step Swings   1 x 10 swings   _____

Core Lifts   Weight Used

Lunges   3 x 5 reps   _____

Bench Press   3 x 5 reps   _____

Auxiliary Lifts   Weight Used

Lat Pulls   2 x 8 reps   _____

Leg Extension   2 x 8 reps   _____

Leg Curls   2 x 8 reps   _____

Neck   2 x 8 reps   _____

Arm Curls   2 x 8 reps   _____

Triceps Extensions   2 x 8 reps   _____

Notes
1) Use a weight you can complete all the repetitions comfortably meaning you could do one or two more at the end of the set.
2) When you could do more than two more repetitions on a set move the weight used up 5 pounds.
3) Rest only 1 minute between sets and no longer.

March

Workout Charts

High School KICKERS
OFF-SEASON Training Calendar
March

SUNDAY	MONDAY	TUESDAY	WEDNESDAY	THURSDAY	FRIDAY	SATURDAY
Week 1 NO WORKOUT REST	Week 1 **Kick** 25 reps into net Ball Contact Kicking Workout Running Workout	Week 1 **Kickers** Quick Feet Drills Weightlifting	Week 1 **Kick** 25 reps into net Ball Contact Kicking Workout Running Workout	Week 1 **Kickers** Quick Feet Drills Weightlifting	Week 1 **Kick** 25 reps into net Ball Contact Kicking Workout Running Workout	Week 1 No training prescribed rest or participate in light physical activity. <u>i.e.</u> basketball, biking, etc.
Week 2 NO WORKOUT REST	Week 2 **Kick** 25 reps into net Ball Contact Kicking Workout Running Workout	Week 2 **Kickers** Quick Feet Drills Weightlifting	Week 2 **Kick** 25 reps into net Ball Contact Kicking Workout Running Workout	Week 2 **Kickers** Quick Feet Drills Weightlifting	Week 2 **Kick** 25 reps into net Ball Contact Kicking Workout Running Workout	Week 2 No training prescribed rest or participate in light physical activity. <u>i.e.</u> basketball, biking, etc.
Week 3 NO WORKOUT REST	Week 3 **Kick** 25 reps into net Ball Contact Kicking Workout Running Workout	Week 3 **Kickers** Quick Feet Drills Weightlifting	Week 3 **Kick** 25 reps into net Ball Contact Kicking Workout Running Workout	Week 3 **Kickers** Quick Feet Drills Weightlifting	Week 3 **Kick** 25 reps into net Ball Contact Kicking Workout Running Workout	Week 3 No training prescribed rest or participate in light physical activity. <u>i.e.</u> basketball, biking, etc.
Week 4 NO WORKOUT REST	Week 4 **Kick** 25 reps outside Ball Contact Kicking Workout Running Workout	Week 4 **Kickers** Quick Feet Drills Weightlifting	Week 4 **Kick** 25 reps into net Ball Contact Kicking Workout Running Workout	Week 4 **Kickers** Quick Feet Drills Weightlifting	Week 4 **Kick** 25 reps into net Ball Contact Kicking Workout Running Workout	Week 4 No training prescribed rest or participate in light physical activity. <u>i.e.</u> basketball, biking, etc.

High School KICKERS
OFF-SEASON SPEED and STRENGTH Training Program
March

MONDAY	TUESDAY	WEDNESDAY	THURSDAY	FRIDAY
Flexibility Agility Warm-up Dynamic Flexibility ------------------------ **Kicker Drills** **1 set of 5** No Step Drill One Step Drill Quick Feet Full Approach Drill **Kicking Workout** 25 Kicks into the NET ------------------------ **Running Workout** 6 x 60 yd sprints – ¾ speed 8 x 40 yd sprints – ¾ speed 45 sec. rest between each	**Flexibility** Agility Warm-up Dynamic Flexibility ---------------------- **Kicker Drills** **1 set of 10** No Step Drill One Step Drill Quick Feet Full Approach Drill ---------------------- **Core Lifts** **3 sets of 8** Cleans Deadlift ---------------------- **Auxiliary Lifts** **2 sets of 8** Glute Ham Raise Push Press Dips	**Flexibility** Agility Warm-up Dynamic Flexibility ------------------------ **Kicker Drills** set of 5 No Step Drill One Step Drill Quick Feet Full Approach Drill **Kicking Workout** 25 Kicks into the NET ------------------------ **Running Workout** 6 x 60 yd sprints – ¾ speed 8 x 40 yd sprints – ¾ speed 45 sec. rest between each	**Flexibility** Agility Warm-up Dynamic Flexibility ---------------------- **Kicker Drills** **1 set of 10** No Step Drill One Step Drill Quick Feet Full Approach Drill ---------------------- **Core Lifts** **3 sets of 8** Squats Bench Press ---------------------- **Auxiliary Lifts** **2 sets of 8** Lat Pulls Leg Extension Leg Curls Neck Arm Curls Tricep Extension	**Flexibility** Agility Warm-up Dynamic Flexibility ------------------------ **Kicker Drills** **1 set of 5** No Step Drill One Step Drill Quick Feet Full Approach Drill **Kicking Workout** 25 Kicks into the NET ------------------------ **Running Workout** 6 x 60 yd sprints – ¾ speed 8 x 40 yd sprints – ¾ speed 45 sec. rest between each

Agility Warm-up Routine
*15 yards – down and back using each movement
High knees
Shuffle
Carioca
Backpedal
Butt kicks
Power skips
Sprint

Dynamic Flexibility Routine
*10 yards–down and back using each movement
Tin soldiers
Walking Hamstring
Knee Tuck/Quad Pull
Front Lunges
Back Lunges
Spiderman

Kicker Workout Recording Sheet

Monday
March Week 1

Flexibility   ### Check when completed

Agility Warm-up   _____
*high knees, shuffle, carioca, backpedal, butt kicks, power skips, spring

Dynamic Flexibility   _____
*tin man, walking hamstring, knee tuck/quad pull, front lunges, back lunges, spiderman

Kicking Without the Ball Drills   ### Check when completed

Quick Feet Full Approach Swings   1 x 5 swings   _____

One-Step Swings   1 x 5 swings   _____

No-Step Swings   1 x 5 swings   _____

Kicking With the Ball Drills   ### Check when completed

At-the-Upright Drill (no step)   5 kicks   _____

Over-the-Upright Drill)one step)   5 kicks   _____

Down-the-Sideline Right sideline (full approach) 5 kicks _____

30 yard field goals middle   10 kicks   _____

Running Workout   ### Time of Run

6 x 60 yard sprints   run ¾ speed for each rep
8 x 40 yard sprints   45 seconds rest in between each run

Notes
1) Use a weight you can complete all the repetitions comfortably meaning you could
   do one or two more at the end of the set.
2) When you could do more than two more repetitions on a set move the weight used up 5 pounds.
3) Rest only 1 minute between sets and no longer.

Kicker Workout Recording Sheet

Tuesday
March Week 1

Flexibility   Check when completed

Agility Warm-up   _____
*high knees, shuffle, carioca, backpedal, butt kicks, power skips, spring

Dynamic Flexibility   _____
*tin man, walking hamstring, knee tuck/quad pull, front lunges, back lunges, spiderman

Kicking Without the Ball Drills   Check when completed

Quick Feet Full Approach Swings	1 x 10 swings	_____
One-Step Swings	1 x 10 swings	_____
No-Step Swings	1 x 10 swings	_____

Core Lifts   Weight Used

Power Cleans	3 x 8 reps	_____
Deadlift	3 x 8 reps	_____

Auxiliary Lifts   Weight Used

Glute Ham Raise	2 x 8 reps	_____
Push Press	2 x 8 reps	_____
Dips	2 x 8 reps	_____

Notes
1) Use a weight you can complete all the repetitions comfortably meaning you could do one or two more at the end of the set.
2) When you could do more than two more repetitions on a set move the weight used up 5 pounds.
3) Rest only 1 minute between sets and no longer.

Kicker Workout Recording Sheet

Wednesday
March Week 1

Flexibility   Check when completed

Agility Warm-up   _____
*high knees, shuffle, carioca, backpedal, butt kicks, power skips, spring

Dynamic Flexibility   _____
*tin man, walking hamstring, knee tuck/quad pull, front lunges, back lunges, spiderman

Kicking Without the Ball Drills   Check when completed

Quick Feet Full Approach Swings   1 x 5 swings   _____

One-Step Swings   1 x 5 swings   _____

No-Step Swings   1 x 5 swings   _____

Kicking With the Ball Drills   Check when completed

At-the-Upright Drill (no step)   5 kicks   _____

Over-the-Upright Drill)one step)   5 kicks   _____

Down-the-Sideline Right sideline (full approach) 5 kicks   _____

30 yard field goals middle   10 kicks   _____

Running Workout   Time of Run

6 x 60 yard sprints   run ¾ speed for each rep
8 x 40 yard sprints   45 seconds rest in between each run

Notes
1) Use a weight you can complete all the repetitions comfortably meaning you could do one or two more at the end of the set.
2) When you could do more than two more repetitions on a set move the weight used up 5 pounds.
3) Rest only 1 minute between sets and no longer.

Kicker Workout Recording Sheet

Thursday
March Week 1

Flexibility   Check when completed

Agility Warm-up   _____
*high knees, shuffle, carioca, backpedal, butt kicks, power skips, spring

Dynamic Flexibility   _____
*tin man, walking hamstring, knee tuck/quad pull, front lunges, back lunges, spiderman

Kicking Without the Ball Drills   Check when completed

Quick Feet Full Approach Swings	1 x 10 swings	_____
One-Step Swings	1 x 10 swings	_____
No-Step Swings	1 x 10 swings	_____

Core Lifts   Weight Used

Squats	3 x 8 reps	_____
Bench Press	3 x 8 reps	_____

Auxiliary Lifts   Weight Used

Lat Pulls	2 x 8 reps	_____
Leg Extension	2 x 8 reps	_____
Leg Curls	2 x 8 reps	_____
Neck	2 x 8 reps	_____
Arm Curls	2 x 8 reps	_____
Triceps Extensions	2 x 8 reps	_____

Notes
1) Use a weight you can complete all the repetitions comfortably meaning you could do one or two more at the end of the set.
2) When you could do more than two more repetitions on a set move the weight used up 5 pounds.
3) Rest only 1 minute between sets and no longer.

Kicker Workout Recording Sheet

Friday
March Week 1

Flexibility	Check when completed

Agility Warm-up   _____
*high knees, shuffle, carioca, backpedal, butt kicks, power skips, spring

Dynamic Flexibility   _____
*tin man, walking hamstring, knee tuck/quad pull, front lunges, back lunges, spiderman

Kicking Without the Ball Drills   Check when completed

Quick Feet Full Approach Swings   1 x 5 swings   _____

One-Step Swings   1 x 5 swings   _____

No-Step Swings   1 x 5 swings   _____

Kicking With the Ball Drills   Check when completed

At-the-Upright Drill (no step)   5 kicks   _____

Over-the-Upright Drill)one step)   5 kicks   _____

Down-the-Sideline Right sideline (full approach) 5 kicks   _____

30 yard field goals middle   10 kicks   _____

Running Workout   Time of Run

6 x 60 yard sprints   run ¾ speed for each rep
8 x 40 yard sprints   45 seconds rest in between each run

Notes
1) Use a weight you can complete all the repetitions comfortably meaning you could do one or two more at the end of the set.
2) When you could do more than two more repetitions on a set move the weight used up 5 pounds.
3) Rest only 1 minute between sets and no longer.

Kicker Workout Recording Sheet

Monday
March Week 2

Flexibility	Check when completed

Agility Warm-up   _____
*high knees, shuffle, carioca, backpedal, butt kicks, power skips, spring

Dynamic Flexibility   _____
*tin man, walking hamstring, knee tuck/quad pull, front lunges, back lunges, spiderman

Kicking Without the Ball Drills   Check when completed

Quick Feet Full Approach Swings	1 x 5 swings	_____
One-Step Swings	1 x 5 swings	_____
No-Step Swings	1 x 5 swings	_____

Kicking With the Ball Drills   Check when completed

At-the-Upright Drill (no step)	5 kicks	_____
Over-the-Upright Drill)one step)	5 kicks	_____
Down-the-Sideline Right sideline (full approach)	5 kicks	_____
30 yard field goals middle	10 kicks	_____

Running Workout   Time of Run

6 x 60 yard sprints   run ¾ speed for each rep
8 x 40 yard sprints   45 seconds rest in between each run

Notes
1) Use a weight you can complete all the repetitions comfortably meaning you could do one or two more at the end of the set.
2) When you could do more than two more repetitions on a set move the weight used up 5 pounds.
3) Rest only 1 minute between sets and no longer.

Kicker Workout Recording Sheet

Tuesday
March Week 2

Flexibility   Check when completed

Agility Warm-up   _____
*high knees, shuffle, carioca, backpedal, butt kicks, power skips, spring

Dynamic Flexibility   _____
*tin man, walking hamstring, knee tuck/quad pull, front lunges, back lunges, spiderman

Kicking Without the Ball Drills   Check when completed

Quick Feet Full Approach Swings	1 x 10 swings	_____
One-Step Swings	1 x 10 swings	_____
No-Step Swings	1 x 10 swings	_____

Core Lifts   Weight Used

Power Cleans	3 x 8 reps	_____
Deadlift	3 x 8 reps	_____

Auxiliary Lifts   Weight Used

Glute Ham Raise	2 x 8 reps	_____
Push Press	2 x 8 reps	_____
Dips	2 x 8 reps	_____

Notes
1) Use a weight you can complete all the repetitions comfortably meaning you could do one or two more at the end of the set.
2) When you could do more than two more repetitions on a set move the weight used up 5 pounds.
3) Rest only 1 minute between sets and no longer.

Kicker Workout Recording Sheet

Wednesday
March Week 2

Flexibility Check when completed

Agility Warm-up   _____
*high knees, shuffle, carioca, backpedal, butt kicks, power skips, spring

Dynamic Flexibility   _____
*tin man, walking hamstring, knee tuck/quad pull, front lunges, back lunges, spiderman

Kicking Without the Ball Drills   Check when completed

Quick Feet Full Approach Swings	1 x 5 swings	_____
One-Step Swings	1 x 5 swings	_____
No-Step Swings	1 x 5 swings	_____

Kicking With the Ball Drills   Check when completed

At-the-Upright Drill (no step)	5 kicks	_____
Over-the-Upright Drill)one step)	5 kicks	_____
Down-the-Sideline Right sideline (full approach)	5 kicks	_____
30 yard field goals middle	10 kicks	_____

Running Workout   Time of Run

6 x 60 yard sprints   run ¾ speed for each rep
8 x 40 yard sprints   45 seconds rest in between each run

Notes
1) Use a weight you can complete all the repetitions comfortably meaning you could do one or two more at the end of the set.
2) When you could do more than two more repetitions on a set move the weight used up 5 pounds.
3) Rest only 1 minute between sets and no longer.

Kicker Workout Recording Sheet

Thursday
March Week 2

Flexibility   Check when completed

Agility Warm-up   _____
*high knees, shuffle, carioca, backpedal, butt kicks, power skips, spring

Dynamic Flexibility   _____
*tin man, walking hamstring, knee tuck/quad pull, front lunges, back lunges, spiderman

Kicking Without the Ball Drills   Check when completed

Quick Feet Full Approach Swings	1 x 10 swings	_____
One-Step Swings	1 x 10 swings	_____
No-Step Swings	1 x 10 swings	_____

Core Lifts   Weight Used

Squats	3 x 8 reps	_____
Bench Press	3 x 8 reps	_____

Auxiliary Lifts   Weight Used

Lat Pulls	2 x 8 reps	_____
Leg Extension	2 x 8 reps	_____
Leg Curls	2 x 8 reps	_____
Neck	2 x 8 reps	_____
Arm Curls	2 x 8 reps	_____
Triceps Extensions	2 x 8 reps	_____

Notes
1) Use a weight you can complete all the repetitions comfortably meaning you could do one or two more at the end of the set.
2) When you could do more than two more repetitions on a set move the weight used up 5 pounds.
3) Rest only 1 minute between sets and no longer.

Kicker Workout Recording Sheet

Friday
March Week 2

Flexibility   ## Check when completed

Agility Warm-up   _____
*high knees, shuffle, carioca, backpedal, butt kicks, power skips, spring

Dynamic Flexibility   _____
*tin man, walking hamstring, knee tuck/quad pull, front lunges, back lunges, spiderman

Kicking Without the Ball Drills   ## Check when completed

Quick Feet Full Approach Swings	1 x 5 swings	_____
One-Step Swings	1 x 5 swings	_____
No-Step Swings	1 x 5 swings	_____

Kicking With the Ball Drills   ## Check when completed

At-the-Upright Drill (no step)	5 kicks	_____
Over-the-Upright Drill)one step)	5 kicks	_____
Down-the-Sideline Right sideline (full approach)	5 kicks	_____
30 yard field goals middle	10 kicks	_____

Running Workout   ## Time of Run

6 x 60 yard sprints   run ¾ speed for each rep
8 x 40 yard sprints   45 seconds rest in between each run

Notes
1) Use a weight you can complete all the repetitions comfortably meaning you could do one or two more at the end of the set.
2) When you could do more than two more repetitions on a set move the weight used up 5 pounds.
3) Rest only 1 minute between sets and no longer.

Kicker Workout Recording Sheet

Monday
March Week 3

Flexibility   Check when completed

Agility Warm-up   _____
*high knees, shuffle, carioca, backpedal, butt kicks, power skips, spring

Dynamic Flexibility   _____
*tin man, walking hamstring, knee tuck/quad pull, front lunges, back lunges, spiderman

Kicking Without the Ball Drills   Check when completed

Quick Feet Full Approach Swings   1 x 5 swings   _____

One-Step Swings   1 x 5 swings   _____

No-Step Swings   1 x 5 swings   _____

Kicking With the Ball Drills   Check when completed

At-the-Upright Drill (no step)   5 kicks   _____

Over-the-Upright Drill)one step)   5 kicks   _____

Down-the-Sideline Right sideline (full approach) 5 kicks   _____

30 yard field goals middle   10 kicks   _____

Running Workout   ### Time of Run

6 x 60 yard sprints   run ¾ speed for each rep
8 x 40 yard sprints   45 seconds rest in between each run

Notes
1) Use a weight you can complete all the repetitions comfortably meaning you could do one or two more at the end of the set.
2) When you could do more than two more repetitions on a set move the weight used up 5 pounds.
3) Rest only 1 minute between sets and no longer.

Kicker Workout Recording Sheet

Tuesday
March Week 3

Flexibility   ### Check when completed

Agility Warm-up   _____
*high knees, shuffle, carioca, backpedal, butt kicks, power skips, spring

Dynamic Flexibility   _____
*tin man, walking hamstring, knee tuck/quad pull, front lunges, back lunges, spiderman

Kicking Without the Ball Drills   ### Check when completed

Quick Feet Full Approach Swings	1 x 10 swings	_____
One-Step Swings	1 x 10 swings	_____
No-Step Swings	1 x 10 swings	_____

Core Lifts   ### Weight Used

Power Cleans	3 x 8 reps	_____
Deadlift	3 x 8 reps	_____

Auxiliary Lifts   ### Weight Used

Glute Ham Raise	2 x 8 reps	_____
Push Press	2 x 8 reps	_____
Dips	2 x 8 reps	_____

Notes
1) Use a weight you can complete all the repetitions comfortably meaning you could do one or two more at the end of the set.
2) When you could do more than two more repetitions on a set move the weight used up 5 pounds.
3) Rest only 1 minute between sets and no longer.

Kicker Workout Recording Sheet

Wednesday
March Week 3

Flexibility   ### Check when completed

Agility Warm-up   _____
*high knees, shuffle, carioca, backpedal, butt kicks, power skips, spring

Dynamic Flexibility   _____
*tin man, walking hamstring, knee tuck/quad pull, front lunges, back lunges, spiderman

Kicking Without the Ball Drills   ### Check when completed

Quick Feet Full Approach Swings   1 x 5 swings   _____

One-Step Swings   1 x 5 swings   _____

No-Step Swings   1 x 5 swings   _____

Kicking With the Ball Drills   ### Check when completed

At-the-Upright Drill (no step)   5 kicks   _____

Over-the-Upright Drill)one step)   5 kicks   _____

Down-the-Sideline Right sideline (full approach) 5 kicks _____

30 yard field goals middle   10 kicks   _____

Running Workout   ### Time of Run

6 x 60 yard sprints   run ¾ speed for each rep
8 x 40 yard sprints   45 seconds rest in between each run

Notes
1) Use a weight you can complete all the repetitions comfortably meaning you could do one or two more at the end of the set.
2) When you could do more than two more repetitions on a set move the weight used up 5 pounds.
3) Rest only 1 minute between sets and no longer.

Kicker Workout Recording Sheet

Thursday
March Week 3

Flexibility		Check when completed

Agility Warm-up _____
*high knees, shuffle, carioca, backpedal, butt kicks, power skips, spring

Dynamic Flexibility _____
*tin man, walking hamstring, knee tuck/quad pull, front lunges, back lunges, spiderman

Kicking Without the Ball Drills — Check when completed

Quick Feet Full Approach Swings	1 x 10 swings	_____
One-Step Swings	1 x 10 swings	_____
No-Step Swings	1 x 10 swings	_____

Core Lifts — Weight Used

Squats	3 x 8 reps	_____
Bench Press	3 x 8 reps	_____

Auxiliary Lifts — Weight Used

Lat Pulls	2 x 8 reps	_____
Leg Extension	2 x 8 reps	_____
Leg Curls	2 x 8 reps	_____
Neck	2 x 8 reps	_____
Arm Curls	2 x 8 reps	_____
Triceps Extensions	2 x 8 reps	_____

Notes
1) Use a weight you can complete all the repetitions comfortably meaning you could do one or two more at the end of the set.
2) When you could do more than two more repetitions on a set move the weight used up 5 pounds.
3) Rest only 1 minute between sets and no longer.

Kicker Workout Recording Sheet

Friday
March Week 3

Flexibility	Check when completed

Agility Warm-up   _____
*high knees, shuffle, carioca, backpedal, butt kicks, power skips, spring

Dynamic Flexibility   _____
*tin man, walking hamstring, knee tuck/quad pull, front lunges, back lunges, spiderman

Kicking Without the Ball Drills   Check when completed

Quick Feet Full Approach Swings	1 x 5 swings	_____
One-Step Swings	1 x 5 swings	_____
No-Step Swings	1 x 5 swings	_____

Kicking With the Ball Drills   Check when completed

At-the-Upright Drill (no step)	5 kicks	_____
Over-the-Upright Drill)one step)	5 kicks	_____
Down-the-Sideline Right sideline (full approach) 5 kicks		_____
30 yard field goals middle	10 kicks	_____

Running Workout   Time of Run

6 x 60 yard sprints   run ¾ speed for each rep
8 x 40 yard sprints   45 seconds rest in between each run

Notes
1) Use a weight you can complete all the repetitions comfortably meaning you could do one or two more at the end of the set.
2) When you could do more than two more repetitions on a set move the weight used up 5 pounds.
3) Rest only 1 minute between sets and no longer.

Kicker Workout Recording Sheet

Monday
March Week 4

Flexibility   ### Check when completed

Agility Warm-up   _____
*high knees, shuffle, carioca, backpedal, butt kicks, power skips, spring

Dynamic Flexibility   _____
*tin man, walking hamstring, knee tuck/quad pull, front lunges, back lunges, spiderman

Kicking Without the Ball Drills   ### Check when completed

Quick Feet Full Approach Swings	1 x 5 swings	_____
One-Step Swings	1 x 5 swings	_____
No-Step Swings	1 x 5 swings	_____

Kicking With the Ball Drills   ### Check when completed

At-the-Upright Drill (no step)	5 kicks	_____
Over-the-Upright Drill)one step)	5 kicks	_____
Down-the-Sideline Right sideline (full approach)	5 kicks	_____
30 yard field goals middle	10 kicks	_____

Running Workout   ### Time of Run

6 x 60 yard sprints   run ¾ speed for each rep
8 x 40 yard sprints   45 seconds rest in between each run

Notes
1) Use a weight you can complete all the repetitions comfortably meaning you could do one or two more at the end of the set.
2) When you could do more than two more repetitions on a set move the weight used up 5 pounds.
3) Rest only 1 minute between sets and no longer.

Kicker Workout Recording Sheet

Tuesday
March Week 4

Flexibility   ### Check when completed

Agility Warm-up   _____
*high knees, shuffle, carioca, backpedal, butt kicks, power skips, spring

Dynamic Flexibility   _____
*tin man, walking hamstring, knee tuck/quad pull, front lunges, back lunges, spiderman

Kicking Without the Ball Drills   ### Check when completed

Quick Feet Full Approach Swings   1 x 10 swings   _____

One-Step Swings   1 x 10 swings   _____

No-Step Swings   1 x 10 swings   _____

Core Lifts   ### Weight Used

Power Cleans   3 x 8 reps   _____

Deadlift   3 x 8 reps   _____

Auxiliary Lifts   ### Weight Used

Glute Ham Raise   2 x 8 reps   _____

Push Press   2 x 8 reps   _____

Dips   2 x 8 reps   _____

Notes
1) Use a weight you can complete all the repetitions comfortably meaning you could do one or two more at the end of the set.
2) When you could do more than two more repetitions on a set move the weight used up 5 pounds.
3) Rest only 1 minute between sets and no longer.

Kicker Workout Recording Sheet

Wednesday
March Week 4

Flexibility	Check when completed

Agility Warm-up _____
*high knees, shuffle, carioca, backpedal, butt kicks, power skips, spring

Dynamic Flexibility _____
*tin man, walking hamstring, knee tuck/quad pull, front lunges, back lunges, spiderman

Kicking Without the Ball Drills — Check when completed

Quick Feet Full Approach Swings	1 x 5 swings	_____
One-Step Swings	1 x 5 swings	_____
No-Step Swings	1 x 5 swings	_____

Kicking With the Ball Drills — Check when completed

At-the-Upright Drill (no step)	5 kicks	_____
Over-the-Upright Drill)one step)	5 kicks	_____
Down-the-Sideline Right sideline (full approach)	5 kicks	_____
30 yard field goals middle	10 kicks	_____

Running Workout

6 x 60 yard sprints
8 x 40 yard sprints

Time of Run

run ¾ speed for each rep
45 seconds rest in between each run

Notes
1) Use a weight you can complete all the repetitions comfortably meaning you could do one or two more at the end of the set.
2) When you could do more than two more repetitions on a set move the weight used up 5 pounds.
3) Rest only 1 minute between sets and no longer.

Kicker Workout Recording Sheet

Thursday
March Week 4

Flexibility   ### Check when completed

Agility Warm-up   _____
*high knees, shuffle, carioca, backpedal, butt kicks, power skips, spring

Dynamic Flexibility   _____
*tin man, walking hamstring, knee tuck/quad pull, front lunges, back lunges, spiderman

Kicking Without the Ball Drills   ### Check when completed

Quick Feet Full Approach Swings   1 x 10 swings   _____

One-Step Swings   1 x 10 swings   _____

No-Step Swings   1 x 10 swings   _____

Core Lifts   ### Weight Used

Squats   3 x 8 reps   _____

Bench Press   3 x 8 reps   _____

Auxiliary Lifts   ### Weight Used

Lat Pulls   2 x 8 reps   _____

Leg Extension   2 x 8 reps   _____

Leg Curls   2 x 8 reps   _____

Neck   2 x 8 reps   _____

Arm Curls   2 x 8 reps   _____

Triceps Extensions   2 x 8 reps   _____

Notes
1) Use a weight you can complete all the repetitions comfortably meaning you could do one or two more at the end of the set.
2) When you could do more than two more repetitions on a set move the weight used up 5 pounds.
3) Rest only 1 minute between sets and no longer.

Kicker Workout Recording Sheet

Friday
March Week 4

Flexibility   Check when completed

Agility Warm-up   _____
*high knees, shuffle, carioca, backpedal, butt kicks, power skips, spring

Dynamic Flexibility   _____
*tin man, walking hamstring, knee tuck/quad pull, front lunges, back lunges, spiderman

Kicking Without the Ball Drills   Check when completed

Quick Feet Full Approach Swings   1 x 5 swings   _____

One-Step Swings   1 x 5 swings   _____

No-Step Swings   1 x 5 swings   _____

Kicking With the Ball Drills   Check when completed

At-the-Upright Drill (no step)   5 kicks   _____

Over-the-Upright Drill)one step)   5 kicks   _____

Down-the-Sideline Right sideline (full approach) 5 kicks _____

30 yard field goals middle   10 kicks   _____

Running Workout   ### Time of Run

6 x 60 yard sprints   run ¾ speed for each rep
8 x 40 yard sprints   45 seconds rest in between each run

Notes
  1) Use a weight you can complete all the repetitions comfortably meaning you could
      do one or two more at the end of the set.
  2) When you could do more than two more repetitions on a set move the weight used up 5 pounds.
  3) Rest only 1 minute between sets and no longer.

April

Kicking Workout Charts

High School KICKERS
OFF-SEASON Training Calendar
April

SUNDAY	MONDAY	TUESDAY	WEDNESDAY	THURSDAY	FRIDAY	SATURDAY
Week 1 NO WORKOUT REST	Week 1 **Kick** 25 reps outside Game Winning Field Goal Workout Running Workout	Week 1 **Kickers** Quick Feet Drills Weightlifting	Week 1 **Kick** 25 reps outside Game Winning Field Goal Workout Running Workout	Week 1 **Kickers** Quick Feet Drills Weightlifting	Week 1 **Kick** 25 reps outside Game Winning Field Goal Workout Running Workout	Week 1 No training prescribed rest or participate in light physical activity. <u>i.e.</u> basketball, biking, etc.
Week 2 NO WORKOUT REST	Week 2 **Kick** 25 reps outside Game Winning Field Goal Workout Running Workout	Week 2 **Kickers** Quick Feet Drills Weightlifting	Week 2 **Kick** 25 reps outside Game Winning Field Goal Workout Running Workout	Week 2 **Kickers** Quick Feet Drills Weightlifting	Week 2 **Kick** 25 reps outside Game Winning Field Goal Workout Running Workout	Week 2 No training prescribed rest or participate in light physical activity. <u>i.e.</u> basketball, biking, etc.
Week 3 NO WORKOUT REST	Week 3 **Kick** 25 reps outside Game Winning Field Goal Workout Running Workout	Week 3 **Kickers** Quick Feet Drills Weightlifting	Week 3 **Kick** 25 reps outside Game Winning Field Goal Workout Running Workout	Week 3 **Kickers** Quick Feet Drills Weightlifting	Week 3 **Kick** 25 reps outside Game Winning Field Goal Workout Running Workout	Week 3 No training prescribed rest or participate in light physical activity. <u>i.e.</u> basketball, biking, etc.
Week 4 NO WORKOUT REST	Week 4 **Kick** 25 reps outside Game Winning Field Goal Workout Running Workout	Week 4 **Kickers** Quick Feet Drills Weightlifting	Week 4 **Kick** 25 reps outside Game Winning Field Goal Workout Running Workout	Week 4 **Kickers** Quick Feet Drills Weightlifting	Week 4 **Kick** 25 reps outside Game Winning Field Goal Workout Running Workout	Week 4 No training prescribed rest or participate in light physical activity. <u>i.e.</u> basketball, biking, etc.

High School KICKERS
OFF-SEASON SPEED and STRENGTH Training Program
April

MONDAY	TUESDAY	WEDNESDAY	THURSDAY	FRIDAY
Flexibility Agility Warm-up Dynamic Flexibility ------------------ **Kicker Drills** **1 set of 5** No Step Drill One Step Drill Quick Feet Full Approach Drill **Kicking Workout** 25 Kicks outside ------------------ **Running Workout** 4 x 60 yd sprints – ¾ speed 6 x 40 yd sprints – ¾ speed 4 x 20 yd sprints – ¾ speed 45 sec. rest between each	**Flexibility** Agility Warm-up Dynamic Flexibility ------------------ **Kicker Drills** **1 set of 10** No Step Drill One Step Drill Quick Feet Full Approach Drill ------------------ **Core Lifts** **3 sets of 5** Cleans Deadlift ------------------ **Auxiliary Lifts** **2 sets of 8** Glute Ham Raise Push Press Dips	**Flexibility** Agility Warm-up Dynamic Flexibility ------------------ **Kicker Drills** **1 set of 5** No Step Drill One Step Drill Quick Feet Full Approach Drill **Kicking Workout** 25 Kicks outside ------------------ **Running Workout** 4 x 60 yd sprints – ¾ speed 6 x 40 yd sprints – ¾ speed 4 x 20 yd sprints – ¾ speed 45 sec. rest between each	**Flexibility** Agility Warm-up Dynamic Flexibility ------------------ **Kicker Drills** **1 set of 10** No Step Drill One Step Drill Quick Feet Full Approach Drill ------------------ **Core Lifts** **3 sets of 5** Squats Bench Press ------------------ **Auxiliary Lifts** **2 sets of 8** Lat Pulls Leg Extension Leg Curls Neck Arm Curls Tricep Extension	**Flexibility** Agility Warm-up Dynamic Flexibility ------------------ --- **Kicker Drills** **1 set of 5** No Step Drill One Step Drill Quick Feet Full Approach Drill **Kicking Workout** 25 Kicks outside ------------------ --- **Running Workout** 4 x 60 yd sprints – ¾ speed 6 x 40 yd sprints – ¾ speed 4 x 20 yd sprints – ¾ speed 45 sec. rest between each

Agility Warm-up Routine
*15 yards – down and back using each movement
High knees
Shuffle
Carioca
Backpedal
Butt kicks
Power skips
Sprint

Dynamic Flexibility Routine
*10 yards – down and back using each movement
Tin soldiers
Walking Hamstring
Knee Tuck/Quad Pull
Front Lunges
Back Lunges
Spiderman

Kicking Workout Chart
Game Winning Field Goals

Left Hash	Middle	Right Hash	Kickoffs
1) __ 30 __	11) __ 30 __	21) __ 30 __	1) _____, _____
2) __ 32 __	12) __ 32 __	22) __ 32 __	2) _____, _____
3) __ 35 __	13) __ 35 __	23) __ 35 __	3) _____, _____
4) __ 38 __	14) __ 38 __	24) __ 38 __	4) _____, _____
5) __ 40 __	15) __ 40 __	25) __ 40 __	5) _____,_____
6) __ 42 __	16) __ 42 __	26) __ 42 __	Hang Time, Distance
7) __ 45 __		27) __ 45 __	

Date: Monday, April Week 1

Field Goals: _____ - 20

Left Hash: _____ - 7   Middle: _____ - 6   Right Hash: _____ - 7

Kickoffs: 5

Kicker Workout Recording Sheet

Tuesday
April Week 1

Flexibility	Check when completed
Agility Warm-up	_____
Dynamic Flexibility	_____

Kicking Without the Ball Drills		Check when completed
No-Step Swings	1 x 10 swings	_____
One-Step Swings	1 x 10 swings	_____
Quick Feet Full Approach Swings	1 x 10 swings	_____

Core Lifts		Weight Used
Power Cleans	3 x 5 reps	_____
Deadlift	3 x 5 reps	_____

Auxiliary Lifts		Weight Used
Glute Ham Raise	2 x 8 reps	_____
Push Press	2 x 8 reps	_____
Dips	2 x 8 reps	_____

Notes
1) Use a weight you can complete all the repetitions comfortably meaning you could do one or two more at the end of the set.
2) When you could do more than two more repetitions on a set move the weight used up 5 pounds.
3) Rest only 1 minute between sets and no longer.

Kicking Workout Chart
Game Winning Field Goals

Left Hash	Middle	Right Hash	Kickoffs
1) __ 30 __	11) __ 30 __	21) __ 30 __	1) _____, _____
2) __ 32 __	12) __ 32 __	22) __ 32 __	2) _____, _____
3) __ 35 __	13) __ 35 __	23) __ 35 __	3) _____, _____
4) __ 38 __	14) __ 38 __	24) __ 38 __	4) _____, _____
5) __ 40 __	15) __ 40 __	25) __ 40 __	5) _____,_____
6) __ 42 __	16) __ 42 __	26) __ 42 __	Hang Time, Distance
7) __ 45 __		27) __ 45 __	

Date: Wednesday, April Week 1

Field Goals: _____ - 20

Left Hash: _____ - 7   Middle: _____ - 6   Right Hash: _____ - 7

Kickoffs: 5

Kicker Workout Recording Sheet

Thursday
April Week 1

Flexibility

	Check when completed
Agility Warm-up	_____
Dynamic Flexibility	_____

Kicking Without the Ball Drills

		Check when completed
No-Step Swings	1 x 10 swings	_____
One-Step Swings	1 x 10 swings	_____
Quick Feet Full Approach Swings	1 x 10 swings	_____

Core Lifts

		Weight Used
Squats	3 x 5 reps	_____
Bench Press	3 x 5 reps	_____

Auxiliary Lifts

		Weight Used
Lat Pulls	2 x 8 reps	_____
Leg Extension	2 x 8 reps	_____
Leg Curls	2 x 8 reps	_____
Neck	2 x 8 reps	_____
Arm Curls	2 x 8 reps	_____
Triceps Extensions	2 x 8 reps	_____

Notes
1) Use a weight you can complete all the repetitions comfortably meaning you could do one or two more at the end of the set.
2) When you could do more than two more repetitions on a set move the weight used up 5 pounds.
3) Rest only 1 minute between sets and no longer.

Kicking Workout Chart
Game Winning Field Goals

Left Hash	Middle	Right Hash	Kickoffs
1) __ 30 __	11) __ 30 __	21) __ 30 __	1) _____, _____
2) __ 32 __	12) __ 32 __	22) __ 32 __	2) _____, _____
3) __ 35 __	13) __ 35 __	23) __ 35 __	3) _____, _____
4) __ 38 __	14) __ 38 __	24) __ 38 __	4) _____, _____
5) __ 40 __	15) __ 40 __	25) __ 40 __	5) _____,_____
6) __ 42 __	16) __ 42 __	26) __ 42 __	Hang Time, Distance
7) __ 45 __		27) __ 45 __	

Date: Friday, April Week 1

Field Goals: _____ - 20

Left Hash: _____ - 7   Middle: _____ - 6   Right Hash: _____ - 7

Kickoffs: 5

April
Weekly Kicking Chart Summary

Dates: April Week 1

Weekly Kicking Performance Summary

DISTANCE		Percent		Field Goal ACCURACY		Percent
20-24: ____ - 0		0 %		Left Hash: ____ - 21		_____
25-29 ____ - 0		0 %		Middle: ____ - 18		_____
30-34: ____ - 18		_____		Right Hash: ____ - 21		_____
35-39: ____ - 18		_____				
40-44: ____ - 18		_____		**KICKOFFS**		
45-49: ____ - 6		_____		Number: 15		
50+: ____ - 0		0 %		Avg. Hang Time: _____		
				Avg. Distance: _____		

TOTALS

Field Goals: _____ - 60

FG % _____

L = Left Hash
M = Middle
R = Right Hash

*Plot all this weeks field goals on the goal posts.
Use L for the left hash field goals, use R for the right hash field goals and M for field goals from the middle.

Game Winning Field Goals

Left Hash	Middle	Right Hash	Kickoffs
1) __ 30 __	11) __ 30 __	21) __ 30 __	1) _____, _____
2) __ 32 __	12) __ 32 __	22) __ 32 __	2) _____, _____
3) __ 35 __	13) __ 35 __	23) __ 35 __	3) _____, _____
4) __ 38 __	14) __ 38 __	24) __ 38 __	4) _____, _____
5) __ 40 __	15) __ 40 __	25) __ 40 __	5) _____, _____
6) __ 42 __	16) __ 42 __	26) __ 42 __	Hang Time, Distance
7) __ 45 __		27) __ 45 __	

Date: Monday, April Week 2

Field Goals: _____ - 20

Left Hash: _____ - 7   Middle: _____ - 6   Right Hash: _____ - 7

Kickoffs: 5

Kicker Workout Recording Sheet

Tuesday
April Week 2

Flexibility   Check when completed

Agility Warm-up   _____

Dynamic Flexibility   _____

Kicking Without the Ball Drills   Check when completed

No-Step Swings   1 x 10 swings   _____

One-Step Swings   1 x 10 swings   _____

Quick Feet Full Approach Swings   1 x 10 swings   _____

Core Lifts   Weight Used

Power Cleans   3 x 5 reps   _____

Deadlift   3 x 5 reps   _____

Auxiliary Lifts   Weight Used

Glute Ham Raise   2 x 8 reps   _____

Push Press   2 x 8 reps   _____

Dips   2 x 8 reps   _____

Notes
1)   Use a weight you can complete all the repetitions comfortably meaning you could do one or two more at the end of the set.
2)   When you could do more than two more repetitions on a set move the weight used up 5 pounds.
3)   Rest only 1 minute between sets and no longer.

Kicking Workout Chart
Game Winning Field Goals

Left Hash	Middle	Right Hash	Kickoffs
1) __ 30 __	11) __ 30 __	21) __ 30 __	1) _____, _____
2) __ 32 __	12) __ 32 __	22) __ 32 __	2) _____, _____
3) __ 35 __	13) __ 35 __	23) __ 35 __	3) _____, _____
4) __ 38 __	14) __ 38 __	24) __ 38 __	4) _____, _____
5) __ 40 __	15) __ 40 __	25) __ 40 __	5) _____, _____
6) __ 42 __	16) __ 42 __	26) __ 42 __	Hang Time, Distance
7) __ 45 __		27) __ 45 __	

Date: Wednesday, April Week 2

Field Goals: _____ - 20

Left Hash: _____ - 7   Middle: _____ - 6   Right Hash: _____ - 7

Kickoffs: 5

Kicker Workout Recording Sheet

Thursday
April Week 2

Flexibility

Check when completed

Agility Warm-up   _____

Dynamic Flexibility   _____

Kicking Specific Drills

Check when completed

No-Step Swings	1 x 10 swings	_____
One-Step Swings	1 x 10 swings	_____
Quick Feet Full Approach Swings	1 x 10 swings	_____

Core Lifts

Weight Used

Squats	3 x 5 reps	_____
Bench Press	3 x 5 reps	_____

Auxiliary Lifts

Weight Used

Lat Pulls	2 x 8 reps	_____
Leg Extension	2 x 8 reps	_____
Leg Curls	2 x 8 reps	_____
Neck	2 x 8 reps	_____
Arm Curls	2 x 8 reps	_____
Triceps Extensions	2 x 8 reps	_____

Notes
1) Use a weight you can complete all the repetitions comfortably meaning you could do one or two more at the end of the set.
2) When you could do more than two more repetitions on a set move the weight used up 5 pounds.
3) Rest only 1 minute between sets and no longer.

Kicking Workout Chart
Game Winning Field Goals

Left Hash	Middle	Right Hash	Kickoffs
1) __ 30 __	11) __ 30 __	21) __ 30 __	1) _____, _____
2) __ 32 __	12) __ 32 __	22) __ 32 __	2) _____, _____
3) __ 35 __	13) __ 35 __	23) __ 35 __	3) _____, _____
4) __ 38 __	14) __ 38 __	24) __ 38 __	4) _____, _____
5) __ 40 __	15) __ 40 __	25) __ 40 __	5) _____,_____
6) __ 42 __	16) __ 42 __	26) __ 42 __	Hang Time, Distance
7) __ 45 __		27) __ 45 __	

Date: Friday, April Week 2

Field Goals: _____ - 20

Left Hash: _____ - 7   Middle: _____ - 6   Right Hash: _____ - 7

Kickoffs: 5

April
Weekly Kicking Chart Summary

Dates: April Week 2

Weekly Kicking Performance Summary

DISTANCE		**Percent**
20-24: _____ - 0		0 %
25-29: _____ - 0		0 %
30-34: _____ - 18		_____
35-39: _____ - 18		_____
40-44: _____ - 18		_____
45-49: _____ - 6		_____
50+: _____ - 0		0 %

Field Goal ACCURACY		**Percent**
Left Hash: _____ - 21		_____
Middle: _____ - 18		_____
Right Hash: _____ - 21		_____

KICKOFFS

Number: 15

Avg. Hang Time: _____

Avg. Distance: _____

TOTALS

Field Goals: _____ - 60

FG % _____

L = Left Hash
M = Middle
R = Right Hash

*Plot all this weeks field goals on the goal posts.
Use L for the left hash field goals, use R for the right hash field goals
and M for field goals from the middle.

Kicking Workout Chart
Game Winning Field Goals

Left Hash	Middle	Right Hash	Kickoffs
1) __ 30 __	11) __ 30 __	21) __ 30 __	1) _____, _____
2) __ 32 __	12) __ 32 __	22) __ 32 __	2) _____, _____
3) __ 35 __	13) __ 35 __	23) __ 35 __	3) _____, _____
4) __ 38 __	14) __ 38 __	24) __ 38 __	4) _____, _____
5) __ 40 __	15) __ 40 __	25) __ 40 __	5) _____, _____
6) __ 42 __	16) __ 42 __	26) __ 42 __	Hang Time, Distance
7) __ 45 __		27) __ 45 __	

Date: Monday, April Week 3

Field Goals: _____ - 20

Left Hash: _____ - 7   Middle: _____ - 6   Right Hash: _____ - 7

Kickoffs: 5

Kicker Workout Recording Sheet

Tuesday
April Week 3

Flexibility

Agility Warm-up

Dynamic Flexibility

Check when completed

_____

_____

Kicking Specific Drills

No-Step Swings

One-Step Swings

Quick Feet Full Approach Swings

1 x 10 swings

1 x 10 swings

1 x 10 swings

Check when completed

_____

_____

_____

Core Lifts

Power Cleans

Deadlift

3 x 5 reps

3 x 5 reps

Weight Used

_____

_____

Auxiliary Lifts

Glute Ham Raise

Push Press

Dips

2 x 8 reps

2 x 8 reps

2 x 8 reps

Weight Used

_____

_____

_____

Notes
1) Use a weight you can complete all the repetitions comfortably meaning you could do one or two more at the end of the set.
2) When you could do more than two more repetitions on a set move the weight used up 5 pounds.
3) Rest only 1 minute between sets and no longer.

Game Winning Field Goals

Left Hash	Middle	Right Hash	Kickoffs
1) __ 30 __	11) __ 30 __	21) __ 30 __	1) _____, _____
2) __ 32 __	12) __ 32 __	22) __ 32 __	2) _____, _____
3) __ 35 __	13) __ 35 __	23) __ 35 __	3) _____, _____
4) __ 38 __	14) __ 38 __	24) __ 38 __	4) _____, _____
5) __ 40 __	15) __ 40 __	25) __ 40 __	5) _____,_____
6) __ 42 __	16) __ 42 __	26) __ 42 __	Hang Time, Distance
7) __ 45 __		27) __ 45 __	

Date: Wednesday, April Week 3

Field Goals: _____ - 20

Left Hash: _____ - 7   Middle: _____ - 6   Right Hash: _____ - 7

Kickoffs: 5

Kicker Workout Recording Sheet

Thursday
April Week 3

Flexibility		Check when completed
Agility Warm-up		_____
Dynamic Flexibility		_____

Kicking Specific Drills		Check when completed
No-Step Swings	1 x 10 swings	_____
One-Step Swings	1 x 10 swings	_____
Quick Feet Full Approach Swings	1 x 10 swings	_____

Core Lifts		Weight Used
Squats	3 x 5 reps	_____
Bench Press	3 x 5 reps	_____

Auxiliary Lifts		Weight Used
Lat Pulls	2 x 8 reps	_____
Leg Extension	2 x 8 reps	_____
Leg Curls	2 x 8 reps	_____
Neck	2 x 8 reps	_____
Arm Curls	2 x 8 reps	_____
Triceps Extensions	2 x 8 reps	_____

Notes
1) Use a weight you can complete all the repetitions comfortably meaning you could do one or two more at the end of the set.
2) When you could do more than two more repetitions on a set move the weight used up 5 pounds.
3) Rest only 1 minute between sets and no longer.

Game Winning Field Goals

Left Hash	Middle	Right Hash	Kickoffs
1) __ 30 __	11) __ 30 __	21) __ 30 __	1) _____, _____
2) __ 32 __	12) __ 32 __	22) __ 32 __	2) _____, _____
3) __ 35 __	13) __ 35 __	23) __ 35 __	3) _____, _____
4) __ 38 __	14) __ 38 __	24) __ 38 __	4) _____, _____
5) __ 40 __	15) __ 40 __	25) __ 40 __	5) _____,_____
6) __ 42 __	16) __ 42 __	26) __ 42 __	Hang Time, Distance
7) __ 45 __		27) __ 45 __	

Date: Friday, April Week 3

Field Goals: ____ - 20

Left Hash: _____ - 7   Middle: _____ - 6   Right Hash: _____ - 7

Kickoffs: 5

April
Weekly Kicking Chart Summary

Dates: April ·Week 3

Weekly Kicking Performance Summary

DISTANCE		Percent	Field Goal ACCURACY		Percent
20-24:	_____ - 0	0 %	Left Hash:	_____ - 21	_____
25-29:	_____ - 0	0 %	Middle:	_____ - 18	_____
30-34:	_____ - 18	_____	Right Hash:	_____ - 21	_____
35-39:	_____ - 18	_____			
40-44:	_____ - 18	_____	**KICKOFFS**		
45-49:	_____ - 6	_____	Number: 15		
50+:	_____ - 0	0 %	Avg. Hang Time: _____		
			Avg. Distance: _____		

TOTALS

Field Goals: _____ - 60

FG % _____

L = Left Hash
M = Middle
R = Right Hash

*Plot all this weeks field goals on the goal posts.
Use L for the left hash field goals, use R for the right hash field goals
and M for field goals from the middle.

Kicking Workout Chart
Game Winning Field Goals

Left Hash	Middle	Right Hash	Kickoffs
1) __ 30 __	11) __ 30 __	21) __ 30 __	1) _____, _____
2) __ 32 __	12) __ 32 __	22) __ 32 __	2) _____, _____
3) __ 35 __	13) __ 35 __	23) __ 35 __	3) _____, _____
4) __ 38 __	14) __ 38 __	24) __ 38 __	4) _____, _____
5) __ 40 __	15) __ 40 __	25) __ 40 __	5) _____,_____
6) __ 42 __	16) __ 42 __	26) __ 42 __	Hang Time, Distance
7) __ 45 __		27) __ 45 __	

Date: Monday, April Week 4

Field Goals: _____ - 20

Left Hash: _____ - 7   Middle: _____ - 6   Right Hash: _____ - 7

Kickoffs: 5

Kicker Workout Recording Sheet

Tuesday
April Week 4

Flexibility   Check when completed

Agility Warm-up   _____

Dynamic Flexibility   _____

Kicking Specific Drills   Check when completed

No-Step Swings   1 x 10 swings   _____

One-Step Swings   1 x 10 swings   _____

Quick Feet Full Approach Swings   1 x 10 swings   _____

Core Lifts   Weight Used

Power Cleans   3 x 5 reps   _____

Deadlift   3 x 5 reps   _____

Auxiliary Lifts   Weight Used

Glute Ham Raise   2 x 8 reps   _____

Push Press   2 x 8 reps   _____

Dips   2 x 8 reps   _____

Notes
1) Use a weight you can complete all the repetitions comfortably meaning you could do one or two more at the end of the set.
2) When you could do more than two more repetitions on a set move the weight used up 5 pounds.
3) Rest only 1 minute between sets and no longer.

Kicking Workout Chart
Game Winning Field Goals

Left Hash	Middle	Right Hash	Kickoffs
1) __ 30 __	11) __ 30 __	21) __ 30 __	1) _____ , _____
2) __ 32 __	12) __ 32 __	22) __ 32 __	2) _____ , _____
3) __ 35 __	13) __ 35 __	23) __ 35 __	3) _____ , _____
4) __ 38 __	14) __ 38 __	24) __ 38 __	4) _____ , _____
5) __ 40 __	15) __ 40 __	25) __ 40 __	5) _____ ,_____
6) __ 42 __	16) __ 42 __	26) __ 42 __	Hang Time, Distance
7) __ 45 __		27) __ 45 __	

Date: Wednesday, April Week 4

Field Goals: _____ - 20

Left Hash: _____ - 7   Middle: _____ - 6   Right Hash: _____ - 7

Kickoffs: 5

Kicker Workout Recording Sheet

Thursday
April Week 4

Flexibility   ### Check when completed

Agility Warm-up   _____

Dynamic Flexibility   _____

Kicking Specific Drills   ### Check when completed

No-Step Swings   1 x 10 swings   _____

One-Step Swings   1 x 10 swings   _____

Quick Feet Full Approach Swings   1 x 10 swings   _____

Core Lifts   ### Weight Used

Squats   3 x 5 reps   _____

Bench Press   3 x 5 reps   _____

Auxiliary Lifts   ### Weight Used

Lat Pulls   2 x 8 reps   _____

Leg Extension   2 x 8 reps   _____

Leg Curls   2 x 8 reps   _____

Neck   2 x 8 reps   _____

Arm Curls   2 x 8 reps   _____

Triceps Extensions   2 x 8 reps   _____

Notes
1) Use a weight you can complete all the repetitions comfortably meaning you could do one or two more at the end of the set.
2) When you could do more than two more repetitions on a set move the weight used up 5 pounds.
3) Rest only 1 minute between sets and no longer.

Game Winning Field Goals

Left Hash	Middle	Right Hash	Kickoffs
1) __ 30 __	11) __ 30 __	21) __ 30 __	1) _____, _____
2) __ 32 __	12) __ 32 __	22) __ 32 __	2) _____, _____
3) __ 35 __	13) __ 35 __	23) __ 35 __	3) _____, _____
4) __ 38 __	14) __ 38 __	24) __ 38 __	4) _____, _____
5) __ 40 __	15) __ 40 __	25) __ 40 __	5) _____, _____
6) __ 42 __	16) __ 42 __	26) __ 42 __	Hang Time, Distance
7) __ 45 __		27) __ 45 __	

Date: Friday, April Week 4

Field Goals: ____ - 20

Left Hash: _____ - 7   Middle: _____ - 6   Right Hash: _____ - 7

Kickoffs: 5

April
Weekly Kicking Chart Summary

Dates: April Week 4

Weekly Kicking Performance Summary

DISTANCE		Percent
20-24: _____ - 0		0 %
25-29: _____ - 0		0 %
30-34: _____ - 18		_____
35-39: _____ - 18		_____
40-44: _____ - 18		_____
45-49: _____ - 6		_____
50+: _____ - 0		0 %

Field Goal ACCURACY		Percent
Left Hash: _____ - 21		_____
Middle: _____ - 18		_____
Right Hash: _____ - 21		_____

KICKOFFS

Number: 15

Avg. Hang Time: _____

Avg. Distance: _____

TOTALS

Field Goals: _____ - 60

FG % _____

L = Left Hash
M = Middle
R = Right Hash

*Plot all this weeks field goals on the goal posts.
Use L for the left hash field goals, use R for the right hash field goals
and M for field goals from the middle.

April Weeks 1-4
MONTHLY Kicking Chart Summary

Dates: April Weeks 1-4

MONTHLY Kicking Performance Summary

DISTANCE		Percent	Field Goal ACCURACY			Percent
20-24:	_____ - 0	0 %	Left Hash:	_____ -	84	_____
25-29:	_____ - 0	0 %	Middle:	_____ -	72	_____
30-34:	_____ - 72	_____	Right Hash:	_____ -	84	_____
35-39:	_____ - 72	_____				
40-44:	_____ - 72	_____				
45-49:	_____ - 24	_____				
50+:	_____ - 0	0 %				

KICKOFFS

Number: 60

Avg. Hang Time: _____

Avg. Distance: _____

TOTALS

Field Goals: _____ - 240

FG % _____

May

Kicking Workout Charts

High School KICKERS
OFF-SEASON Training Calendar
May

SUNDAY	MONDAY	TUESDAY	WEDNESDAY	THURSDAY	FRIDAY	SATURDAY
Week 1 NO WORKOUT REST	Week 1 **Kick** 25 reps outside Long Distance Field Goal Workout Running Workout	Week 1 **Kickers** Quick Feet Drills Weightlifting	Week 1 **Kick** 25 reps outside Long Distance Field Goal Workout Running Workout	Week 1 **Kickers** Quick Feet Drills Weightlifting	Week 1 **Kick** 25 reps outside Long Distance Field Goal Workout Running Workout	Week 1 No training prescribed rest or participate in light physical activity. <u>i.e.</u> basketball, biking, etc.
Week 2 NO WORKOUT REST	Week 2 **Kick** 25 reps outside Long Distance Field Goal Workout Running Workout	Week 2 **Kickers** Quick Feet Drills Weightlifting	Week 2 **Kick** 25 reps outside Long Distance Field Goal Workout Running Workout	Week 2 **Kickers** Quick Feet Drills Weightlifting	Week 2 **Kick** 25 reps outside Long Distance Field Goal Workout Running Workout	Week 2 No training prescribed rest or participate in light physical activity. <u>i.e.</u> basketball, biking, etc.
Week 3 NO WORKOUT REST	Week 3 **Kick** 25 reps outside Long Distance Field Goal Workout Running Workout	Week 3 **Kickers** Quick Feet Drills Weightlifting	Week 3 **Kick** 25 reps outside Long Distance Field Goal Workout Running Workout	Week 3 **Kickers** Quick Feet Drills Weightlifting	Week 3 **Kick** 25 reps outside Long Distance Field Goal Workout Running Workout	Week 3 No training prescribed rest or participate in light physical activity. <u>i.e.</u> basketball, biking, etc.
Week 4 NO WORKOUT REST	Week 4 **Kick** 25 reps outside Long Distance Field Goal Workout Running Workout	Week 4 **Kickers** Quick Feet Drills Weightlifting	Week 4 **Kick** 25 reps outside Long Distance Field Goal Workout Running Workout	Week 4 **Kickers** Quick Feet Drills Weightlifting	Week 4 **Kick** 25 reps outside Long Distance Field Goal Workout Running Workout	Week 4 No training prescribed rest or participate in light physical activity. <u>i.e.</u> basketball, biking, etc.

High School KICKERS
OFF-SEASON SPEED and STRENGTH Training Program
May

MONDAY	TUESDAY	WEDNESDAY	THURSDAY	FRIDAY
Flexibility Agility Warm-up Dynamic Flexibility ------------------------ **Kicker Drills** **1 set of 5** No Step Drill One Step Drill Quick Feet Full Approach Drill **Kicking Workout** 25 Kicks outside ------------------------ **Running Workout** 2 x 60 yd sprints – ¾ speed 4 x 40 yd sprints – ¾ speed 6 x 20 yd sprints – ¾ speed 4 x 10 yd sprints – ¾ speed 45 sec. rest between each	**Flexibility** Agility Warm-up Dynamic Flexibility ------------------------ **Kicker Drills** **1 set of 10** No Step Drill One Step Drill Quick Feet Full Approach Drill ------------------------ **Core Lifts** **3 sets of 8** Cleans Deadlift ------------------------ **Auxiliary Lifts** **2 sets of 8** Glute Ham Raise Push Press Dips	**Flexibility** Agility Warm-up Dynamic Flexibility ------------------------ **Kicker Drills** **1 set of 5** No Step Drill One Step Drill Quick Feet Full Approach Drill **Kicking Workout** 25 Kicks outside ------------------------ **Running Workout** 2 x 60 yd sprints – ¾ speed 4 x 40 yd sprints – ¾ speed 6 x 20 yd sprints – ¾ speed 4 x 10 yd sprints – ¾ speed 45 sec. rest between each	**Flexibility** Agility Warm-up Dynamic Flexibility ------------------------ **Kicker Drills** **1 set of 10** No Step Drill One Step Drill Quick Feet Full Approach Drill ------------------------ **Core Lifts** **3 sets of 8** Squats Bench Press ------------------------ **Auxiliary Lifts** **2 sets of 8** Lat Pulls Leg Extension Leg Curls Neck Arm Curls Tricep Extension	**Flexibility** Agility Warm-up Dynamic Flexibility ------------------------ **Kicker Drills** **1 set of 5** No Step Drill One Step Drill Quick Feet Full Approach Drill **Kicking Workout** 25 Kicks outside ------------------------ **Running Workout** 2 x 60 yd sprints – ¾ speed 4 x 40 yd sprints – ¾ speed 6 x 20 yd sprints – ¾ speed 4 x 10 yd sprints – ¾ speed 45 sec. rest between each

Agility Warm-up Routine
*15 yards – down and back using each movement
High knees
Shuffle
Carioca
Backpedal
Butt kicks
Power skips
Sprint

Dynamic Flexibility Routine
*10 yards–down and back using each movement
Tin soldiers
Walking Hamstring
Knee Tuck/Quad Pull
Front Lunges
Back Lunges
Spiderman

Long Distance Field Goals

Left Hash	Middle	Right Hash	Kickoffs
1) __ 35 __	11) __ 35 __	21) __ 35 __	1) _____ , _____
2) __ 37 __	12) __ 37 __	22) __ 37 __	2) _____ , _____
3) __ 40 __	13) __ 40 __	23) __ 40 __	3) _____ , _____
4) __ 42 __	14) __ 42 __	24) __ 42 __	4) _____ , _____
5) __ 45 __	15) __ 45 __	25) __ 45 __	5) _____ , _____
6) __ 47 __	16) __ 50 __	26) __ 47 __	Hang Time, Distance
7) __ 50 __		**27)** __ 50 __	

Date: Monday, May Week 1

Field Goals: _____ - 20

Left Hash: _____ - 7   Middle: _____ - 6   Right Hash: _____ - 7

Kickoffs: 5

Kicker Workout Recording Sheet

Tuesday
May Week 1

Flexibility

Check when completed

Agility Warm-up _____

Dynamic Flexibility _____

Kicking Specific Drills

Check when completed

No-Step Swings | 1 x 10 swings | _____

One-Step Swings | 1 x 10 swings | _____

Quick Feet Full Approach Swings | 1 x 10 swings | _____

Core Lifts

Weight Used

Power Cleans | 3 x 8 reps | _____

Deadlift | 3 x 8 reps | _____

Auxiliary Lifts

Weight Used

Glute Ham Raise | 2 x 8 reps | _____

Push Press | 2 x 8 reps | _____

Dips | 2 x 8 reps | _____

Notes
1) Use a weight you can complete all the repetitions comfortably meaning you could do one or two more at the end of the set.
2) When you could do more than two more repetitions on a set move the weight used up 5 pounds.
3) Rest only 1 minute between sets and no longer.

Kicking Workout Chart
Long Distance Field Goals

Left Hash	Middle	Right Hash	Kickoffs
1) __ 35 __	11) __ 35 __	21) __ 35 __	1) _____ , _____
2) __ 37 __	12) __ 37 __	22) __ 37 __	2) _____ , _____
3) __ 40 __	13) __ 40 __	23) __ 40 __	3) _____ , _____
4) __ 42 __	14) __ 42 __	24) __ 42 __	4) _____ , _____
5) __ 45 __	15) __ 45 __	25) __ 45 __	5) _____ , _____
6) __ 47 __	16) __ 50 __	26) __ 47 __	Hang Time, Distance
7) __ 50 __		27) __ 50 __	

Date: Wednesday, May Week 1

Field Goals: _____ - 20

Left Hash: _____ - 7   Middle: _____ - 6   Right Hash: _____ - 7

Kickoffs: 5

Kicker Workout Recording Sheet

Thursday
May Week 1

Flexibility   Check when completed

Agility Warm-up   _____

Dynamic Flexibility   _____

Kicking Specific Drills   Check when completed

No-Step Swings   1 x 10 swings   _____

One-Step Swings   1 x 10 swings   _____

Quick Feet Full Approach Swings   1 x 10 swings   _____

Core Lifts   Weight Used

Squats   3 x 8 reps   _____

Bench Press   3 x 8 reps   _____

Auxiliary Lifts   Weight Used

Lat Pulls   2 x 8 reps   _____

Leg Extension   2 x 8 reps   _____

Leg Curls   2 x 8 reps   _____

Neck   2 x 8 reps   _____

Arm Curls   2 x 8 reps   _____

Triceps Extensions   2 x 8 reps   _____

Notes
1) Use a weight you can complete all the repetitions comfortably meaning you could do one or two more at the end of the set.
2) When you could do more than two more repetitions on a set move the weight used up 5 pounds.
3) Rest only 1 minute between sets and no longer.

Kicking Workout Chart
Long Distance Field Goals

Left Hash	Middle	Right Hash	Kickoffs
1) __ 35 __	11) __ 35 __	21) __ 35 __	1) _____, _____
2) __ 37 __	12) __ 37 __	22) __ 37 __	2) _____, _____
3) __ 40 __	13) __ 40 __	23) __ 40 __	3) _____, _____
4) __ 42 __	14) __ 42 __	24) __ 42 __	4) _____, _____
5) __ 45 __	15) __ 45 __	25) __ 45 __	5) _____,_____
6) __ 47 __	16) __ 50 __	26) __ 47 __	Hang Time, Distance
7) __ 50 __		27) __ 50 __	

Date: Friday, May Week 1

Field Goals: _____ - 20

Left Hash: _____ - 7   Middle: _____ - 6   Right Hash: _____ - 7

Kickoffs: 5

May
Weekly Kicking Chart Summary

Dates: May Week 1

Weekly Kicking Performance Summary

DISTANCE		Percent		Field Goal ACCURACY		Percent
20-24:	_____ - 0	0 %		Left Hash:	_____ - 21	_____
25-29:	_____ - 0	0 %		Middle:	_____ - 18	_____
30-34:	_____ - 0	0 %		Right Hash:	_____ - 21	_____
35-39:	_____ - 18	_____				
40-44:	_____ - 18	_____				
45-49:	_____ - 15	_____				
50+:	_____ - 9	_____				

KICKOFFS

Number: 15

Avg. Hang Time: _____

Avg. Distance: _____

TOTALS

Field Goals: _____ - 60

FG % _____

L = Left Hash
M = Middle
R = Right Hash

*Plot all this weeks field goals on the goal posts.
Use L for the left hash field goals, use R for the right hash field goals and M for field goals from the middle.

Kicking Workout Chart
Long Distance Field Goals

Left Hash	Middle	Right Hash	Kickoffs
1) __ 35 __	11) __ 35 __	21) __ 35 __	1) _____, _____
2) __ 37 __	12) __ 37 __	22) __ 37 __	2) _____, _____
3) __ 40 __	13) __ 40 __	23) __ 40 __	3) _____, _____
4) __ 42 __	14) __ 42 __	24) __ 42 __	4) _____, _____
5) __ 45 __	15) __ 45 __	25) __ 45 __	5) _____, _____
6) __ 47 __	16) __ 50 __	26) __ 47 __	Hang Time, Distance
7) __ 50 __		27) __ 50 __	

Date: Monday, May Week 2

Field Goals: _____ - 20

Left Hash: _____ - 7   Middle: _____ - 6   Right Hash: _____ - 7

Kickoffs: 5

Kicker Workout Recording Sheet

Tuesday
May Week 2

Flexibility   Check when completed

Agility Warm-up   _____

Dynamic Flexibility   _____

Kicking Specific Drills   Check when completed

No-Step Swings   1 x 10 swings   _____

One-Step Swings   1 x 10 swings   _____

Quick Feet Full Approach Swings   1 x 10 swings   _____

Core Lifts   Weight Used

Power Cleans   3 x 8 reps   _____

Deadlift   3 x 8 reps   _____

Auxiliary Lifts   Weight Used

Glute Ham Raise   2 x 8 reps   _____

Push Press   2 x 8 reps   _____

Dips   2 x 8 reps   _____

Notes
1) Use a weight you can complete all the repetitions comfortably meaning you could do one or two more at the end of the set.
2) When you could do more than two more repetitions on a set move the weight used up 5 pounds.
3) Rest only 1 minute between sets and no longer.

Long Distance Field Goals

Left Hash	Middle	Right Hash	Kickoffs
1) __ 35 __	11) __ 35 __	21) __ 35 __	1) _____, _____
2) __ 37 __	12) __ 37 __	22) __ 37 __	2) _____, _____
3) __ 40 __	13) __ 40 __	23) __ 40 __	3) _____, _____
4) __ 42 __	14) __ 42 __	24) __ 42 __	4) _____, _____
5) __ 45 __	15) __ 45 __	25) __ 45 __	5) _____, _____
6) __ 47 __	16) __ 50 __	26) __ 47 __	Hang Time, Distance
7) __ 50 __		27) __ 50 __	

Date: Wednesday, May Week 2

Field Goals: _____ - 20

Left Hash: _____ - 7   Middle: _____ - 6   Right Hash: _____ - 7

Kickoffs: 5

Kicker Workout Recording Sheet

Thursday
May Week 2

Flexibility   ### Check when completed

Agility Warm-up   _____

Dynamic Flexibility   _____

Kicking Specific Drills   ### Check when completed

No-Step Swings	1 x 10 swings	_____
One-Step Swings	1 x 10 swings	_____
Quick Feet Full Approach Swings	1 x 10 swings	_____

Core Lifts   ### Weight Used

| Squats | 3 x 8 reps | _____ |
| Bench Press | 3 x 8 reps | _____ |

Auxiliary Lifts   ### Weight Used

Lat Pulls	2 x 8 reps	_____
Leg Extension	2 x 8 reps	_____
Leg Curls	2 x 8 reps	_____
Neck	2 x 8 reps	_____
Arm Curls	2 x 8 reps	_____
Triceps Extensions	2 x 8 reps	_____

Notes
1) Use a weight you can complete all the repetitions comfortably meaning you could do one or two more at the end of the set.
2) When you could do more than two more repetitions on a set move the weight used up 5 pounds.
3) Rest only 1 minute between sets and no longer.

Long Distance Field Goals

Left Hash	Middle	Right Hash	Kickoffs
1) __ 35 __	11) __ 35 __	21) __ 35 __	1) _____, _____
2) __ 37 __	12) __ 37 __	22) __ 37 __	2) _____, _____
3) __ 40 __	13) __ 40 __	23) __ 40 __	3) _____, _____
4) __ 42 __	14) __ 42 __	24) __ 42 __	4) _____, _____
5) __ 45 __	15) __ 45 __	25) __ 45 __	5) _____, _____
6) __ 47 __	16) __ 50 __	26) __ 47 __	Hang Time, Distance
7) __ 50 __		27) __ 50 __	

Date: Friday, May Week 2

Field Goals: _____ - 20

Left Hash: _____ - 7   Middle: _____ - 6   Right Hash: _____ - 7

Kickoffs: 5

May
Weekly Kicking Chart Summary

Dates: May Week 2

Weekly Kicking Performance Summary

DISTANCE		**Percent**	**Field Goal ACCURACY**		**Percent**
20-24: _____	- 0	0 %	Left Hash: _____	- 21	_____
25-29: _____	- 0	0 %	Middle: _____	- 18	_____
30-34 _____	- 0	0 %	Right Hash: _____	- 21	_____
35-39: _____	- 18	_____			
40-44: _____	- 18	_____			
45-49: _____	- 15	_____			
50+: _____	- 9	_____			

KICKOFFS

Number: 15

Avg. Hang Time: _____

Avg. Distance: _____

TOTALS

Field Goals: _____ - 60

FG % _____

L = Left Hash
M = Middle
R = Right Hash

*Plot all this weeks field goals on the goal posts.
Use L for the left hash field goals, use R for the right hash field goals
and M for field goals from the middle.

Kicking Workout Chart
Long Distance Field Goals

Left Hash	Middle	Right Hash	Kickoffs
1) __ 35 __	11) __ 35 __	21) __ 35 __	1) _____, _____
2) __ 37 __	12) __ 37 __	22) __ 37 __	2) _____, _____
3) __ 40 __	13) __ 40 __	23) __ 40 __	3) _____, _____
4) __ 42 __	14) __ 42 __	24) __ 42 __	4) _____, _____
5) __ 45 __	15) __ 45 __	25) __ 45 __	5) _____,_____
6) __ 47 __	16) __ 50 __	26) __ 47 __	Hang Time, Distance
7) __ 50 __		27) __ 50 __	

Date: Monday, May Week 3

Field Goals: _____ - 20

Left Hash: _____ - 7   Middle: _____ - 6   Right Hash: _____ - 7

Kickoffs: 5

Kicker Workout Recording Sheet

Tuesday
May Week 3

Flexibility

Check when completed

Agility Warm-up   _____

Dynamic Flexibility   _____

Kicking Specific Drills

Check when completed

No-Step Swings	1 x 10 swings	_____
One-Step Swings	1 x 10 swings	_____
Quick Feet Full Approach Swings	1 x 10 swings	_____

Core Lifts

Weight Used

| Power Cleans | 3 x 8 reps | _____ |
| Deadlift | 3 x 8 reps | _____ |

Auxiliary Lifts

Weight Used

Glute Ham Raise	2 x 8 reps	_____
Push Press	2 x 8 reps	_____
Dips	2 x 8 reps	_____

Notes
1) Use a weight you can complete all the repetitions comfortably meaning you could do one or two more at the end of the set.
2) When you could do more than two more repetitions on a set move the weight used up 5 pounds.
3) Rest only 1 minute between sets and no longer.

Long Distance Field Goals

Left Hash	Middle	Right Hash	Kickoffs
1) __ 35 __	11) __ 35 __	21) __ 35 __	1) _____ , _____
2) __ 37 __	12) __ 37 __	22) __ 37 __	2) _____ , _____
3) __ 40 __	13) __ 40 __	23) __ 40 __	3) _____ , _____
4) __ 42 __	14) __ 42 __	24) __ 42 __	4) _____ , _____
5) __ 45 __	15) __ 45 __	25) __ 45 __	5) _____ , _____
6) __ 47 __	16) __ 50 __	26) __ 47 __	Hang Time, Distance
7) __ 50 __		27) __ 50 __	

Date: Wednesday, May Week 3

Field Goals: _____ - 20

Left Hash: _____ - 7   Middle: _____ - 6   Right Hash: _____ - 7

Kickoffs: 5

Kicker Workout Recording Sheet

Thursday
May Week 3

Flexibility

Check when completed

Agility Warm-up   _____

Dynamic Flexibility   _____

Kicking Specific Drills

Check when completed

Exercise	Sets/Reps	Check
No-Step Swings	1 x 10 swings	_____
One-Step Swings	1 x 10 swings	_____
Quick Feet Full Approach Swings	1 x 10 swings	_____

Core Lifts

Weight Used

Exercise	Sets/Reps	Weight
Squats	3 x 8 reps	_____
Bench Press	3 x 8 reps	_____

Auxiliary Lifts

Weight Used

Exercise	Sets/Reps	Weight
Lat Pulls	2 x 8 reps	_____
Leg Extension	2 x 8 reps	_____
Leg Curls	2 x 8 reps	_____
Neck	2 x 8 reps	_____
Arm Curls	2 x 8 reps	_____
Triceps Extensions	2 x 8 reps	_____

Notes
1) Use a weight you can complete all the repetitions comfortably meaning you could do one or two more at the end of the set.
2) When you could do more than two more repetitions on a set move the weight used up 5 pounds.
3) Rest only 1 minute between sets and no longer.

Long Distance Field Goals

Left Hash	Middle	Right Hash	Kickoffs
1) __ 35 __	11) __ 35 __	21) __ 35 __	1) _____, _____
2) __ 37 __	12) __ 37 __	22) __ 37 __	2) _____, _____
3) __ 40 __	13) __ 40 __	23) __ 40 __	3) _____, _____
4) __ 42 __	14) __ 42 __	24) __ 42 __	4) _____, _____
5) __ 45 __	15) __ 45 __	25) __ 45 __	5) _____,_____
6) __ 47 __	16) __ 50 __	26) __ 47 __	Hang Time, Distance
7) __ 50 __		27) __ 50 __	

Date: Friday, May Week 3

Field Goals: ____ - 20

Left Hash: _____ - 7   Middle: _____ - 6   Right Hash: _____ - 7

Kickoffs: 5

May
Weekly Kicking Chart Summary

Dates: May Week 3

Weekly Kicking Performance Summary

DISTANCE		Percent
20-24: _____ - 0		0 %
25-29: _____ - 0		0 %
30-34: _____ - 0		0 %
35-39: _____ - 18		_____
40-44: _____ - 18		_____
45-49: _____ - 15		_____
50+: _____ - 9		_____

Field Goal ACCURACY	Percent
Left Hash: _____ - 21	_____
Middle: _____ - 18	_____
Right Hash: _____ - 21	_____

KICKOFFS

Number: 15

Avg. Hang Time: _____

Avg. Distance: _____

TOTALS

Field Goals: _____ - 60

FG % _____

L = Left Hash
M = Middle
R = Right Hash

*Plot all this weeks field goals on the goal posts.
Use L for the left hash field goals, use R for the right hash field goals
and M for field goals from the middle.

Kicking Workout Chart
Long Distance Field Goals

Left Hash	Middle	Right Hash	Kickoffs
1) __ 35 __	11) __ 35 __	21) __ 35 __	1) _____, _____
2) __ 37 __	12) __ 37 __	22) __ 37 __	2) _____, _____
3) __ 40 __	13) __ 40 __	23) __ 40 __	3) _____, _____
4) __ 42 __	14) __ 42 __	24) __ 42 __	4) _____, _____
5) __ 45 __	15) __ 45 __	25) __ 45 __	5) _____,_____
6) __ 47 __	16) __ 50 __	26) __ 47 __	Hang Time, Distance
7) __ 50 __		27) __ 50 __	

Date: Monday, May Week 4

Field Goals: _____ - 20

Left Hash: _____ - 7   Middle: _____ - 6   Right Hash: _____ - 7

Kickoffs: 5

Kicker Workout Recording Sheet

Tuesday
May Week 4

Flexibility   ### Check when completed

Agility Warm-up   _____

Dynamic Flexibility   _____

Kicking Specific Drills   ### Check when completed

No-Step Swings   1 x 10 swings   _____

One-Step Swings   1 x 10 swings   _____

Quick Feet Full Approach Swings 1 x 10 swings   _____

Core Lifts   ### Weight Used

Power Cleans   3 x 8 reps   _____

Deadlift   3 x 8 reps   _____

Auxiliary Lifts   ### Weight Used

Glute Ham Raise   2 x 8 reps   _____

Push Press   2 x 8 reps   _____

Dips   2 x 8 reps   _____

Notes
1)   Use a weight you can complete all the repetitions comfortably meaning you could do one or two more at the end of the set.
2)   When you could do more than two more repetitions on a set move the weight used up 5 pounds.
3)   Rest only 1 minute between sets and no longer.

Kicking Workout Chart
Long Distance Field Goals

Left Hash	Middle	Right Hash	Kickoffs
1) __ 35 __	11) __ 35 __	21) __ 35 __	1) _____ , _____
2) __ 37 __	12) __ 37 __	22) __ 37 __	2) _____ , _____
3) __ 40 __	13) __ 40 __	23) __ 40 __	3) _____ , _____
4) __ 42 __	14) __ 42 __	24) __ 42 __	4) _____ , _____
5) __ 45 __	15) __ 45 __	25) __ 45 __	5) _____ ,_____
6) __ 47 __	16) __ 50 __	26) __ 47 __	Hang Time, Distance
7) __ 50 __		27) __ 50 __	

Date: Wednesday, May Week 4

Field Goals: _____ - 20

Left Hash: _____ - 7   Middle: _____ - 6   Right Hash: _____ - 7

Kickoffs: 5

131

Kicker Workout Recording Sheet

Thursday
May Week 4

Flexibility

Check when completed

Agility Warm-up _____

Dynamic Flexibility _____

Kicking Specific Drills

Check when completed

No-Step Swings   1 x 10 swings   _____

One-Step Swings   1 x 10 swings   _____

Quick Feet Full Approach Swings   1 x 10 swings   _____

Core Lifts

Weight Used

Squats   3 x 8 reps   _____

Bench Press   3 x 8 reps   _____

Auxiliary Lifts

Weight Used

Lat Pulls   2 x 8 reps   _____

Leg Extension   2 x 8 reps   _____

Leg Curls   2 x 8 reps   _____

Neck   2 x 8 reps   _____

Arm Curls   2 x 8 reps   _____

Triceps Extensions   2 x 8 reps   _____

Notes
1) Use a weight you can complete all the repetitions comfortably meaning you could do one or two more at the end of the set.
2) When you could do more than two more repetitions on a set move the weight used up 5 pounds.
3) Rest only 1 minute between sets and no longer.

Kicking Workout Chart
Long Distance Field Goals

Left Hash	Middle	Right Hash	Kickoffs
1) __ 35 __	11) __ 35 __	21) __ 35 __	1) _____, _____
2) __ 37 __	12) __ 37 __	22) __ 37 __	2) _____, _____
3) __ 40 __	13) __ 40 __	23) __ 40 __	3) _____, _____
4) __ 42 __	14) __ 42 __	24) __ 42 __	4) _____, _____
5) __ 45 __	15) __ 45 __	25) __ 45 __	5) _____,_____
6) __ 47 __	16) __ 50 __	26) __ 47 __	Hang Time, Distance
7) __ 50 __		27) __ 50 __	

Date: Friday, May Week 4

Field Goals: _____ - 20

Left Hash: _____ - 7   Middle: _____ - 6   Right Hash: _____ - 7

Kickoffs: 5

133

May
Weekly Kicking Chart Summary

Dates: May Week 4

Weekly Kicking Performance Summary

DISTANCE		Percent	Field Goal ACCURACY		Percent
20-24:	_____ - 0	0 %	Left Hash: _____ - 21		_____
25-29:	_____ - 0	0 %	Middle: _____ - 18		_____
30-34:	_____ - 0	0 %	Right Hash: _____ - 21		_____
35-39:	_____ - 18	_____			
40-44:	_____ - 18	_____	**KICKOFFS**		
45-49:	_____ - 15	_____			
50+:	_____ - 9	_____	Number: 15		

Avg. Hang Time: _____

Avg. Distance: _____

TOTALS

Field Goals: _____ - 60

FG % _____

L = Left Hash
M = Middle
R = Right Hash

*Plot all this weeks field goals on the goal posts.
Use L for the left hash field goals, use R for the right hash field goals and M for field goals from the middle.

May
MONTHLY Kicking Chart Summary

Dates: May Weeks 1 – 4

MONTHLY Kicking Performance Summary

DISTANCE	Percent	Field Goal ACCURACY	Percent
20-24: _____ - 0	0 %	Left Hash: _____ - 84	_____
25-29: _____ - 0	0 %	Middle: _____ - 72	_____
30-34: _____ - 0	0 %	Right Hash: _____ - 84	_____
35-39: _____ - 72	_____		
40-44: _____ - 72	_____	**KICKOFFS**	
45-49: _____ - 60	_____	Number: 60	
50+: _____ - 36	_____	Avg. Hang Time: _____	
		Avg. Distance: _____	

TOTALS

Field Goals: _____ - 240

FG % _____

June

Kicking Workout Charts

High School KICKERS
OFF-SEASON Training Calendar
June

SUNDAY	MONDAY	TUESDAY	WEDNESDAY	THURSDAY	FRIDAY	SATURDAY
Week 1 NO WORKOUT REST	Week 1 **Kick** 25 reps outside Game Winning Field Goal Workout Running Workout	Week 1 **Kickers** Quick Feet Drills Weightlifting	Week 1 **Kick** 25 reps outside Long Distance Field Goal Workout Running Workout	Week 1 **Kickers** Quick Feet Drills Weightlifting	Week 1 **Kick** 25 reps outside Game Winning Field Goal Workout Running Workout	Week 1 No training prescribed rest or participate in light physical activity. i.e. basketball, biking, etc.
Week 2 NO WORKOUT REST	Week 2 **Kick** 25 reps outside Long Distance Field Goal Workout Running Workout	Week 2 **Kickers** Quick Feet Drills Weightlifting	Week 2 **Kick** 25 reps outside Game Winning Field Goal Workout Running Workout	Week 2 **Kickers** Quick Feet Drills Weightlifting	Week 2 **Kick** 25 reps outside Long Distance Field Goal Workout Running Workout	Week 2 No training prescribed rest or participate in light physical activity. i.e. basketball, biking, etc.
Week 3 NO WORKOUT REST	Week 3 **Kick** 25 reps outside Game Winning Field Goal Workout Running Workout	Week 3 **Kickers** Quick Feet Drills Weightlifting	Week 3 **Kick** 25 reps outside Long Distance Field Goal Workout Running Workout	Week 3 **Kickers** Quick Feet Drills Weightlifting	Week 3 **Kick** 25 reps outside Game Winning Field Goal Workout Running Workout	Week 3 No training prescribed rest or participate in light physical activity. i.e. basketball, biking, etc.
Week 4 NO WORKOUT REST	Week 4 **Kick** 25 reps outside Long Distance Field Goal Workout Running Workout	Week 4 **Kickers** Quick Feet Drills Weightlifting	Week 4 **Kick** 25 reps outside Running Workout	Week 4 **Kickers** Quick Feet Drills Weightlifting	Week 4 **Kick** 25 reps outside Long Distance Field Goal Workout Running Workout	Week 4 No training prescribed rest or participate in light physical activity. i.e. basketball, biking, etc.
Week 5 NO WORKOUT REST	Week 5 **Kick** 25 reps outside Game Winning Field Goal Workout Running Workout	Week 5 **Kickers** Quick Feet Drills Weightlifting	Week 5 **Kick** 25 reps outside Long Distance Field Goal Workout Running Workout	Week 5 **Kickers** Quick Feet Drills Weightlifting	Week 5 **Kick** 25 reps outside Game Winning Field Goal Workout Running Workout	Week 5 No training prescribed rest or participate in light physical activity. i.e. basketball, biking, etc.

High School KICKERS
OFF-SEASON SPEED and STRENGTH Training Program
June

MONDAY	TUESDAY	WEDNESDAY	THURSDAY	FRIDAY
Flexibility Agility Warm-up Dynamic Flexibility	**Flexibility** Agility Warm-up Dynamic Flexibility	**Flexibility** Agility Warm-up Dynamic Flexibility	**Flexibility** Agility Warm-up Dynamic Flexibility	**Flexibility** Agility Warm-up Dynamic Flexibility
Kicker Drills **1 set of 5** No Step Drill One Step Drill Quick Feet Full Approach Drill	**Kicker Drills** **1 set of 10** No Step Drill One Step Drill Quick Feet Full Approach Drill	**Kicker Drills** **1 set of 5** No Step Drill One Step Drill Quick Feet Full Approach Drill	**Kicker Drills** **1 set of 10** No Step Drill One Step Drill Quick Feet Full Approach Drill	**Kicker Drills** **1 set of 5** No Step Drill One Step Drill Quick Feet Full Approach Drill
Kicking Workout 25 Kicks outside	**Core Lifts** **3 sets of 5** Cleans Deadlift	**Kicking Workout** 25 Kicks outside	**Core Lifts** **3 sets of 5** Squats Bench Press	**Kicking Workout** 25 Kicks outside
Running Workout 2 x 220 yd sprints – ¾ speed 3 minute rest between each 4 x 110 yd sprints – ¾ speed 2 minute rest between each	**Auxiliary Lifts** **2 sets of 8** Glute Ham Raise Push Press Dips	**Running Workout** 2 x 220 yd sprints – ¾ speed 3 minute rest between each 4 x 110 yd sprints – ¾ speed 2 minute rest between each	**Auxiliary Lifts** **2 sets of 8** Lat Pulls Leg Extension Leg Curls Neck Arm Curls Tricep Extension	**Running Workout** 2 x 220 yd sprints – ¾ speed 3 minute rest between each 4 x 110 yd sprints – ¾ speed 2 minute rest between each

Agility Warm-up Routine
*15 yards–down and back using each movement
High knees
Shuffle
Carioca
Backpedal
Butt kicks
Power skips
Sprint

Dynamic Flexibility Routine
*10 yards–down and back using each movement
Tin soldiers
Walking Hamstring
Knee Tuck/Quad Pull
Front Lunges
Back Lunges
Spiderman

Kicking Workout Chart
Game Winning Field Goals

Left Hash	Middle	Right Hash	Kickoffs
1) __ 30 __	11) __ 30 __	21) __ 30 __	1) _____, _____
2) __ 32 __	12) __ 32 __	22) __ 32 __	2) _____, _____
3) __ 35 __	13) __ 35 __	23) __ 35 __	3) _____, _____
4) __ 38 __	14) __ 38 __	24) __ 38 __	4) _____, _____
5) __ 40 __	15) __ 40 __	25) __ 40 __	5) _____, _____
6) __ 42 __	16) __ 42 __	26) __ 42 __	Hang Time, Distance
7) __ 45 __		27) __ 45 __	

Date: Monday, June Week 1

Field Goals: _____ - 20

Left Hash: _____ - 7   Middle: _____ - 6   Right Hash: _____ - 7

Kickoffs: 5

Kicker Workout Recording Sheet

Tuesday

June Week 1

Flexibility		Check when completed
Agility Warm-up		_____
Dynamic Flexibility		_____

Kicking Specific Drills		Check when completed
No-Step Swings	1 x 10 swings	_____
One-Step Swings	1 x 10 swings	_____
Quick Feet Full Approach Swings	1 x 10 swings	_____

Core Lifts		Weight Used
Power Cleans	3 x 5 reps	_____
Deadlift	3 x 5 reps	_____

Auxiliary Lifts		Weight Used
Glute Ham Raise	2 x 8 reps	_____
Push Press	2 x 8 reps	_____
Dips	2 x 8 reps	_____

Notes
1) Use a weight you can complete all the repetitions comfortably meaning you could do one or two more at the end of the set.
2) When you could do more than two more repetitions on a set move the weight used up 5 pounds.
3) Rest only 1 minute between sets and no longer.

Kicking Workout Chart
Long Distance Field Goals

Left Hash	Middle	Right Hash	Kickoffs
1) __ 35 __	11) __ 35 __	21) __ 35 __	1) _____, _____
2) __ 37 __	12) __ 37 __	22) __ 37 __	2) _____, _____
3) __ 40 __	13) __ 40 __	23) __ 40 __	3) _____, _____
4) __ 42 __	14) __ 42 __	24) __ 42 __	4) _____, _____
5) __ 45 __	15) __ 45 __	25) __ 45 __	5) _____,_____
6) __ 47 __	16) __ 50 __	26) __ 47 __	Hang Time, Distance
7) __ 50 __		27) __ 50 __	

Date: Wednesday, June Week 1

Field Goals: _____ - 20

Left Hash: _____ - 7   Middle: _____ - 6   Right Hash: _____ - 7

Kickoffs: 5

Kicker Workout Recording Sheet

Thursday

June Week 1

Flexibility   ### Check when completed

Agility Warm-up   _____

Dynamic Flexibility   _____

Kicking Specific Drills   ### Check when completed

No-Step Swings   1 x 10 swings   _____

One-Step Swings   1 x 10 swings   _____

Quick Feet Full Approach Swings   1 x 10 swings   _____

Core Lifts   ### Weight Used

Squats   3 x 5 reps   _____

Bench Press   3 x 5 reps   _____

Auxiliary Lifts   ### Weight Used

Lat Pulls   2 x 8 reps   _____

Leg Extension   2 x 8 reps   _____

Leg Curls   2 x 8 reps   _____

Neck   2 x 8 reps   _____

Arm Curls   2 x 8 reps   _____

Triceps Extensions   2 x 8 reps   _____

Notes
1) Use a weight you can complete all the repetitions comfortably meaning you could do one or two more at the end of the set.
2) When you could do more than two more repetitions on a set move the weight used up 5 pounds.
3) Rest only 1 minute between sets and no longer.

Kicking Workout Chart
Game Winning Field Goals

Left Hash	Middle	Right Hash	Kickoffs
1) __ 30 __	11) __ 30 __	21) __ 30 __	1) _____ , _____
2) __ 32 __	12) __ 32 __	22) __ 32 __	2) _____ , _____
3) __ 35 __	13) __ 35 __	23) __ 35 __	3) _____ , _____
4) __ 38 __	14) __ 38 __	24) __ 38 __	4) _____ , _____
5) __ 40 __	15) __ 40 __	25) __ 40 __	5) _____ , _____
6) __ 42 __	16) __ 42 __	26) __ 42 __	Hang Time, Distance
7) __ 45 __		27) __ 45 __	

Date: Friday, June Week 1

Field Goals: _____ - 20

Left Hash: _____ - 7   Middle: _____ - 6   Right Hash: _____ - 7

Kickoffs: 5

Weekly Kicking Chart Summary

Dates: June Week 1

Weekly Kicking Performance Summary

DISTANCE		Percent	Field Goal ACCURACY		Percent
20-24: _____ - 0		0 %	Left Hash: _____ - 21		_____
25-29: _____ - 0		0 %	Middle: _____ - 18		_____
30-34: _____ - 12		_____	Right Hash: _____ - 21		_____
35-39: _____ - 18		_____			
40-44: _____ - 18		_____	**KICKOFFS**		
45-49: _____ - 9		_____	Number: 15		
50+: _____ - 3		_____	Avg. Hang Time: _____		
			Avg. Distance: _____		

TOTALS

Field Goals: _____ - 60

FG % _____

L = Left Hash
M = Middle
R = Right Hash

*Plot all this weeks field goals on the goal posts.
Use L for the left hash field goals, use R for the right hash field goals
and M for field goals from the middle.

Kicking Workout Chart
Long Distance Field Goals

Left Hash	Middle	Right Hash	Kickoffs
1) __ 35 __	11) __ 35 __	21) __ 35 __	1) _____, _____
2) __ 37 __	12) __ 37 __	22) __ 37 __	2) _____, _____
3) __ 40 __	13) __ 40 __	23) __ 40 __	3) _____, _____
4) __ 42 __	14) __ 42 __	24) __ 42 __	4) _____, _____
5) __ 45 __	15) __ 45 __	25) __ 45 __	5) _____,_____
6) __ 47 __	16) __ 50 __	26) __ 47 __	Hang Time, Distance
7) __ 50 __		27) __ 50 __	

Date: Monday, June Week 2

Field Goals: _____ - 20

Left Hash: _____ - 7   Middle: _____ - 6   Right Hash: _____ - 7

Kickoffs: 5

Kicker Workout Recording Sheet

Tuesday

June Week 2

Flexibility		Check when completed
Agility Warm-up		_____
Dynamic Flexibility		_____

Kicking Specific Drills		Check when completed
No-Step Swings	1 x 10 swings	_____
One-Step Swings	1 x 10 swings	_____
Quick Feet Full Approach Swings	1 x 10 swings	_____

Core Lifts		Weight Used
Power Cleans	3 x 5 reps	_____
Deadlift	3 x 5 reps	_____

Auxiliary Lifts		Weight Used
Glute Ham Raise	2 x 8 reps	_____
Push Press	2 x 8 reps	_____
Dips	2 x 8 reps	_____

Notes
1) Use a weight you can complete all the repetitions comfortably meaning you could do one or two more at the end of the set.
2) When you could do more than two more repetitions on a set move the weight used up 5 pounds.
3) Rest only 1 minute between sets and no longer.

Kicking Workout Chart
Game Winning Field Goals

Left Hash	Middle	Right Hash	Kickoffs
1) __ 30 __	11) __ 30 __	21) __ 30 __	1) _____, _____
2) __ 32 __	12) __ 32 __	22) __ 32 __	2) _____, _____
3) __ 35 __	13) __ 35 __	23) __ 35 __	3) _____, _____
4) __ 38 __	14) __ 38 __	24) __ 38 __	4) _____, _____
5) __ 40 __	15) __ 40 __	25) __ 40 __	5) _____,_____
6) __ 42 __	16) __ 42 __	26) __ 42 __	Hang Time, Distance
7) __ 45 __		27) __ 45 __	

Date: Wednesday, June Week 2

Field Goals: _____ - 20

Left Hash: _____ - 7   Middle: _____ - 6   Right Hash: _____ - 7

Kickoffs: 5

Kicker Workout Recording Sheet

Thursday

June Week 2

Flexibility

Agility Warm-up

Dynamic Flexibility

Check when completed

_____

_____

Kicking Specific Drills

		Check when completed
No-Step Swings	1 x 10 swings	_____
One-Step Swings	1 x 10 swings	_____
Quick Feet Full Approach Swings	1 x 10 swings	_____

Core Lifts

		Weight Used
Squats	3 x 5 reps	_____
Bench Press	3 x 5 reps	_____

Auxiliary Lifts

		Weight Used
Lat Pulls	2 x 8 reps	_____
Leg Extension	2 x 8 reps	_____
Leg Curls	2 x 8 reps	_____
Neck	2 x 8 reps	_____
Arm Curls	2 x 8 reps	_____
Triceps Extensions	2 x 8 reps	_____

Notes
1) Use a weight you can complete all the repetitions comfortably meaning you could do one or two more at the end of the set.
2) When you could do more than two more repetitions on a set move the weight used up 5 pounds.
3) Rest only 1 minute between sets and no longer.

Kicking Workout Chart
Long Distance Field Goals

Left Hash	Middle	Right Hash	Kickoffs
1) __ 35 __	11) __ 35 __	21) __ 35 __	1) _____ , _____
2) __ 37 __	12) __ 37 __	22) __ 37 __	2) _____ , _____
3) __ 40 __	13) __ 40 __	23) __ 40 __	3) _____ , _____
4) __ 42 __	14) __ 42 __	24) __ 42 __	4) _____ , _____
5) __ 45 __	15) __ 45 __	25) __ 45 __	5) _____ ,_____
6) __ 47 __	16) __ 50 __	26) __ 47 __	Hang Time, Distance
7) __ 50 __		27) __ 50 __	

Date: Friday, June Week 2

Field Goals: _____ - 20

Left Hash: _____ - 7   Middle: _____ - 6   Right Hash: _____ - 7

Kickoffs: 5

Weekly Kicking Chart Summary

Dates: Week 2

Weekly Kicking Performance Summary

DISTANCE		Percent	Field Goal ACCURACY		Percent
20-24:	_____ - 0	0 %	Left Hash:	_____ - 21	_____
25-29:	_____ - 0	0 %	Middle:	_____ - 18	_____
30-34:	_____ - 6	_____	Right Hash:	_____ - 21	_____
35-39:	_____ - 18	_____			
40-44:	_____ - 18	_____			
45-49:	_____ - 12	_____			
50+:	_____ - 6	_____			

KICKOFFS

Number: 15

Avg. Hang Time: _____

Avg. Distance: _____

TOTALS

Field Goals: _____ - 60

FG % _____

L = Left Hash
M = Middle
R = Right Hash

*Plot all this weeks field goals on the goal posts.
Use L for the left hash field goals, use R for the right hash field goals and M for field goals from the middle.

Kicking Workout Chart
Game Winning Field Goals

Left Hash	Middle	Right Hash	Kickoffs
1) __ 30 __	11) __ 30 __	21) __ 30 __	1) _____, _____
2) __ 32 __	12) __ 32 __	22) __ 32 __	2) _____, _____
3) __ 35 __	13) __ 35 __	23) __ 35 __	3) _____, _____
4) __ 38 __	14) __ 38 __	24) __ 38 __	4) _____, _____
5) __ 40 __	15) __ 40 __	25) __ 40 __	5) _____,_____
6) __ 42 __	16) __ 42 __	26) __ 42 __	Hang Time, Distance
7) __ 45 __		27) __ 45 __	

Date: Monday, June Week 3

Field Goals: _____ - 20

Left Hash: _____ - 7   Middle: _____ - 6   Right Hash: _____ - 7

Kickoffs: 5

Kicker Workout Recording Sheet

Tuesday

June Week 3

Flexibility

Check when completed

Agility Warm-up   _____

Dynamic Flexibility   _____

Kicking Specific Drills   Check when completed

No-Step Swings	1 x 10 swings	_____
One-Step Swings	1 x 10 swings	_____
Quick Feet Full Approach Swings	1 x 10 swings	_____

Core Lifts   Weight Used

Power Cleans	3 x 5 reps	_____
Deadlift	3 x 5 reps	_____

Auxiliary Lifts   Weight Used

Glute Ham Raise	2 x 8 reps	_____
Push Press	2 x 8 reps	_____
Dips	2 x 8 reps	_____

Notes
1) Use a weight you can complete all the repetitions comfortably meaning you could do one or two more at the end of the set.
2) When you could do more than two more repetitions on a set move the weight used up 5 pounds.
3) Rest only 1 minute between sets and no longer.

Kicking Workout Chart
Long Distance Field Goals

Left Hash	Middle	Right Hash	Kickoffs
1) __ 35 __	11) __ 35 __	21) __ 35 __	1) _____ , _____
2) __ 37 __	12) __ 37 __	22) __ 37 __	2) _____ , _____
3) __ 40 __	13) __ 40 __	23) __ 40 __	3) _____ , _____
4) __ 42 __	14) __ 42 __	24) __ 42 __	4) _____ , _____
5) __ 45 __	15) __ 45 __	25) __ 45 __	5) _____ , _____
6) __ 47 __	16) __ 50 __	26) __ 47 __	Hang Time, Distance
7) __ 50 __		27) __ 50 __	

Date: Wednesday, June Week 3

Field Goals: ____ - 20

Left Hash: _____ - 7   Middle: _____ - 6   Right Hash: _____ - 7

Kickoffs: 5

Kicker Workout Recording Sheet

Thursday

June 13, 2013

Flexibility		Check when completed
Agility Warm-up		_____
Dynamic Flexibility		_____

Kicking Specific Drills		Check when completed
No-Step Swings	1 x 10 swings	_____
One-Step Swings	1 x 10 swings	_____
Quick Feet Full Approach Swings	1 x 10 swings	_____

Core Lifts		Weight Used
Squats	3 x 5 reps	_____
Bench Press	3 x 5 reps	_____

Auxiliary Lifts		Weight Used
Lat Pulls	2 x 8 reps	_____
Leg Extension	2 x 8 reps	_____
Leg Curls	2 x 8 reps	_____
Neck	2 x 8 reps	_____
Arm Curls	2 x 8 reps	_____
Triceps Extensions	2 x 8 reps	_____

Notes
1) Use a weight you can complete all the repetitions comfortably meaning you could do one or two more at the end of the set.
2) When you could do more than two more repetitions on a set move the weight used up 5 pounds.
3) Rest only 1 minute between sets and no longer.

Kicking Workout Chart
Game Winning Field Goals

	Left Hash		Middle		Right Hash		Kickoffs
1)	__ 30 __	11)	__ 30 __	21)	__ 30 __	1)	_____ , _____
2)	__ 32 __	12)	__ 32 __	22)	__ 32 __	2)	_____ , _____
3)	__ 35 __	13)	__ 35 __	23)	__ 35 __	3)	_____ , _____
4)	__ 38 __	14)	__ 38 __	24)	__ 38 __	4)	_____ , _____
5)	__ 40 __	15)	__ 40 __	25)	__ 40 __	5)	_____ , _____
6)	__ 42 __	16)	__ 42 __	26)	__ 42 __		Hang Time, Distance
7)	__ 45 __			27)	__ 45 __		

Date: Friday, June Week 3

Field Goals: _____ - 20

Left Hash: _____ - 7   Middle: _____ - 6   Right Hash: _____ - 7

Kickoffs: 5

155

June
Weekly Kicking Chart Summary

Dates: June Weeks 1-3

Weekly Kicking Performance Summary

DISTANCE		Percent
20-24: _____ - 0		0 %
25-29: _____ - 0		0 %
30-34: _____ - 12		_____
35-39: _____ - 18		_____
40-44: _____ - 18		_____
45-49: _____ - 9		_____
50+: _____ - 3		_____

Field Goal ACCURACY		Percent
Left Hash: _____ - 21		_____
Middle: _____ - 18		_____
Right Hash: _____ - 21		_____

KICKOFFS

Number: 15

Avg. Hang Time: _____

Avg. Distance: _____

TOTALS

Field Goals: _____ - 60

FG % _____

L = Left Hash
M = Middle
R = Right Hash

*Plot all this weeks field goals on the goal posts.
Use L for the left hash field goals, use R for the right hash field goals
and M for field goals from the middle.

Kicking Workout Chart
Long Distance Field Goals

Left Hash	Middle	Right Hash	Kickoffs
1) __ 35 __	11) __ 35 __	21) __ 35 __	1) _____ , _____
2) __ 37 __	12) __ 37 __	22) __ 37 __	2) _____ , _____
3) __ 40 __	13) __ 40 __	23) __ 40 __	3) _____ , _____
4) __ 42 __	14) __ 42 __	24) __ 42 __	4) _____ , _____
5) __ 45 __	15) __ 45 __	25) __ 45 __	5) _____ , _____
6) __ 47 __	16) __ 50 __	26) __ 47 __	Hang Time, Distance
7) __ 50 __		27) __ 50 __	

Date: Monday, June Week 4

Field Goals: _____ - 20

Left Hash: _____ - 7   Middle: _____ - 6   Right Hash: _____ - 7

Kickoffs: 5

Kicker Workout Recording Sheet

Tuesday

June Week 4

Flexibility		Check when completed
Agility Warm-up		_____
Dynamic Flexibility		_____

Kicking Specific Drills		Check when completed
No-Step Swings	1 x 10 swings	_____
One-Step Swings	1 x 10 swings	_____
Quick Feet Full Approach Swings	1 x 10 swings	_____

Core Lifts		Weight Used
Power Cleans	3 x 5 reps	_____
Deadlift	3 x 5 reps	_____

Auxiliary Lifts		Weight Used
Glute Ham Raise	2 x 8 reps	_____
Push Press	2 x 8 reps	_____
Dips	2 x 8 reps	_____

Notes
1) Use a weight you can complete all the repetitions comfortably meaning you could do one or two more at the end of the set.
2) When you could do more than two more repetitions on a set move the weight used up 5 pounds.
3) Rest only 1 minute between sets and no longer.

Kicking Workout Chart
Game Winning Field Goals

Left Hash	Middle	Right Hash	Kickoffs
1) __ 30 __	11) __ 30 __	21) __ 30 __	1) _____ , _____
2) __ 32 __	12) __ 32 __	22) __ 32 __	2) _____ , _____
3) __ 35 __	13) __ 35 __	23) __ 35 __	3) _____ , _____
4) __ 38 __	14) __ 38 __	24) __ 38 __	4) _____ , _____
5) __ 40 __	15) __ 40 __	25) __ 40 __	5) _____ ,_____
6) __ 42 __	16) __ 42 __	26) __ 42 __	Hang Time, Distance
7) __ 45 __		27) __ 45 __	

Date: Wednesday, June Week 4

Field Goals: _____ - 20

Left Hash: _____ - 7   Middle: _____ - 6   Right Hash: _____ - 7

Kickoffs: 5

Kicker Workout Recording Sheet

Thursday

June Week 4

Flexibility   Check when completed

Agility Warm-up   _____

Dynamic Flexibility   _____

Kicking Specific Drills   Check when completed

No-Step Swings   1 x 10 swings   _____

One-Step Swings   1 x 10 swings   _____

Quick Feet Full Approach Swings   1 x 10 swings   _____

Core Lifts   Weight Used

Squats   3 x 5 reps   _____

Bench Press   3 x 5 reps   _____

Auxiliary Lifts   Weight Used

Lat Pulls   2 x 8 reps   _____

Leg Extension   2 x 8 reps   _____

Leg Curls   2 x 8 reps   _____

Neck   2 x 8 reps   _____

Arm Curls   2 x 8 reps   _____

Triceps Extensions   2 x 8 reps   _____

Notes
1) Use a weight you can complete all the repetitions comfortably meaning you could do one or two more at the end of the set.
2) When you could do more than two more repetitions on a set move the weight used up 5 pounds.
3) Rest only 1 minute between sets and no longer.

Long Distance Field Goals

Left Hash	Middle	Right Hash	Kickoffs
1) __ 35 __	11) __ 35 __	21) __ 35 __	1) _____, _____
2) __ 37 __	12) __ 37 __	22) __ 37 __	2) _____, _____
3) __ 40 __	13) __ 40 __	23) __ 40 __	3) _____, _____
3) __ 42 __	14) __ 42 __	24) __ 42 __	4) _____, _____
4) __ 45 __	15) __ 45 __	25) __ 45 __	5) _____,_____
5) __ 47 __	16) __ 50 __	26) __ 47 __	Hang Time, Distance
6) __ 50 __		27) __ 50 __	

Date: Friday, June Week 4

Field Goals: _____ - 20

Left Hash: _____ - 7   Middle: _____ - 6   Right Hash: _____ - 7

Kickoffs: 5

June
Weekly Kicking Chart Summary

Dates: June Week 4

Weekly Kicking Performance Summary

DISTANCE		Percent	Field Goal ACCURACY		Percent
20-24: _____ - 0		0 %	Left Hash: _____ - 21		_____
25-29: _____ - 0		0 %	Middle: _____ - 18		_____
30-34: _____ - 6		_____	Right Hash: _____ - 21		_____
35-39: _____ - 18		_____			
40-44: _____ - 18		_____	**KICKOFFS**		
45-49: _____ - 12		_____	Number: 15		
50+: _____ - 6		_____	Avg. Hang Time: _____		
			Avg. Distance: _____		

TOTALS

Field Goals: _____ - 60

FG % _____

L = Left Hash
M = Middle
R = Right Hash

*Plot all this weeks field goals on the goal posts.
Use L for the left hash field goals, use R for the right hash field goals and M for field goals from the middle.

Kicking Workout Chart
Game Winning Field Goals

Left Hash	Middle	Right Hash	Kickoffs
1) __ 30 __	11) __ 30 __	21) __ 30 __	1) _____, _____
2) __ 32 __	12) __ 32 __	22) __ 32 __	2) _____, _____
3) __ 35 __	13) __ 35 __	23) __ 35 __	3) _____, _____
4) __ 38 __	14) __ 38 __	24) __ 38 __	4) _____, _____
5) __ 40 __	15) __ 40 __	25) __ 40 __	5) _____,_____
6) __ 42 __	16) __ 42 __	26) __ 42 __	Hang Time, Distance
7) __ 45 __		27) __ 45 __	

Date: Monday, June Week 5

Field Goals: _____ - 20

Left Hash: _____ - 7   Middle: _____ - 6   Right Hash: _____ - 7

Kickoffs: 5

Kicker Workout Recording Sheet

Tuesday

June Week 5

Flexibility		Check when completed
Agility Warm-up		_____
Dynamic Flexibility		_____

Kicking Specific Drills		Check when completed
No-Step Swings	1 x 10 swings	_____
One-Step Swings	1 x 10 swings	_____
Quick Feet Full Approach Swings	1 x 10 swings	_____

Core Lifts		Weight Used
Power Cleans	3 x 5 reps	_____
Deadlift	3 x 5 reps	_____

Auxiliary Lifts		Weight Used
Glute Ham Raise	2 x 8 reps	_____
Push Press	2 x 8 reps	_____
Dips	2 x 8 reps	_____

Notes
1) Use a weight you can complete all the repetitions comfortably meaning you could do one or two more at the end of the set.
2) When you could do more than two more repetitions on a set move the weight used up 5 pounds.
3) Rest only 1 minute between sets and no longer.

Long Distance Field Goals

Left Hash	Middle	Right Hash	Kickoffs
1) __ 35 __	11) __ 35 __	21) __ 35 __	1) _____ , _____
2) __ 37 __	12) __ 37 __	22) __ 37 __	2) _____ , _____
3) __ 40 __	13) __ 40 __	23) __ 40 __	3) _____ , _____
4) __ 42 __	14) __ 42 __	24) __ 42 __	4) _____ , _____
5) __ 45 __	15) __ 45 __	25) __ 45 __	5) _____ ,_____
6) __ 47 __	16) __ 50 __	26) __ 47 __	Hang Time, Distance
7) __ 50 __		27) __ 50 __	

Date: Wednesday, June Week 5

Field Goals: _____ - 20

Left Hash: _____ - 7   Middle: _____ - 6   Right Hash: _____ - 7

Kickoffs: 5

Kicker Workout Recording Sheet

Thursday

June Week 5

Flexibility

Check when completed

Agility Warm-up   _____

Dynamic Flexibility   _____

Kicking Specific Drills

Check when completed

No-Step Swings   1 x 10 swings   _____

One-Step Swings   1 x 10 swings   _____

Quick Feet Full Approach Swings   1 x 10 swings   _____

Core Lifts

Weight Used

Squats   3 x 5 reps   _____

Bench Press   3 x 5 reps   _____

Auxiliary Lifts

Weight Used

Lat Pulls   2 x 8 reps   _____

Leg Extension   2 x 8 reps   _____

Leg Curls   2 x 8 reps   _____

Neck   2 x 8 reps   _____

Arm Curls   2 x 8 reps   _____

Triceps Extensions   2 x 8 reps   _____

Notes
1) Use a weight you can complete all the repetitions comfortably meaning you could do one or two more at the end of the set.
2) When you could do more than two more repetitions on a set move the weight used up 5 pounds.
3) Rest only 1 minute between sets and no longer.

Kicking Workout Chart
Game Winning Field Goals

Left Hash	Middle	Right Hash	Kickoffs
1) __ 30 __	11) __ 30 __	21) __ 30 __	1) _____, _____
2) __ 32 __	12) __ 32 __	22) __ 32 __	2) _____, _____
3) __ 35 __	13) __ 35 __	23) __ 35 __	3) _____, _____
4) __ 38 __	14) __ 38 __	24) __ 38 __	4) _____, _____
5) __ 40 __	15) __ 40 __	25) __ 40 __	5) _____,_____
6) __ 42 __	16) __ 42 __	26) __ 42 __	Hang Time, Distance
7) __ 45 __		27) __ 45 __	

Date: Friday, June Week 5

Field Goals: _____ - 20

Left Hash: _____ - 7   Middle: _____ - 6   Right Hash: _____ - 7

Kickoffs: 5

June
Weekly Kicking Chart Summary

Dates: June Week 5

Weekly Kicking Performance Summary

DISTANCE		Percent		Field Goal ACCURACY		Percent
20-24: _____ - 0		0 %		Left Hash: _____ - 21		_____
25-29: _____ - 0		0 %		Middle: _____ - 18		_____
30-34: _____ - 12		_____		Right Hash: _____ - 21		_____
35-39: _____ - 18		_____				
40-44: _____ - 18		_____		**KICKOFFS**		
45-49: _____ - 9		_____		Number: 15		
50+: _____ - 3		_____		Avg. Hang Time: _____		
				Avg. Distance: _____		

TOTALS

Field Goals: _____ - 60

FG % _____

L = Left Hash
M = Middle
R = Right Hash

*Plot all this weeks field goals on the goal posts.
Use L for the left hash field goals, use R for the right hash field goals and M
for field goals from the middle.

June
MONTHLY Kicking Chart Summary

Dates: June Weeks 1-5

MONTHLY Kicking Performance Summary

DISTANCE		Percent		Field Goal ACCURACY		Percent
20-24:	____ - 0	0 %		Left Hash:	____ - 105	_____
25-29:	____ - 0	0 %		Middle:	____ - 90	_____
30-34:	____ - 48	_____		Right Hash:	____ - 105	_____
35-39:	____ - 90	_____				
40-44:	____ - 90	_____		**KICKOFFS**		
45-49:	____ - 51	_____		Number: 25		
50+:	____ - 21	_____		Avg. Hang Time: ____		
				Avg. Distance: ____		

TOTALS

Field Goals: _____ - 300

FG % _____

July

Kicking Workout Charts

High School KICKERS
OFF-SEASON Training Calendar
July

SUNDAY	MONDAY	TUESDAY	WEDNESDAY	THURSDAY	FRIDAY	SATURDAY
Week 1 NO WORKOUT REST	Week 1 **Kickers** Quick Feet Drills Weightlifting	Week 1 **Kick** 10 reps outside Game Winning Field Goals Workout Running Workout	Week 1 **Kickers** Quick Feet Drills Weightlifting	Week 1 **Kick** 10 reps outside Game Winning Field Goals Workout Running Workout	Week 1 **Kickers** Quick Feet Drills Weightlifting	Week 1 No training prescribed rest or participate in light physical activity. i.e. basketball, biking, etc.
Week 2 NO WORKOUT REST	Week 2 **Kickers** Quick Feet Drills Weightlifting	Week 2 **Kick** 10 reps outside Game Winning Field Goals Workout Running Workout	Week 2 **Kickers** Quick Feet Drills Weightlifting	Week 2 **Kick** 10 reps outside Game Winning Field Goals Workout Running Workout	Week 2 **Kickers** Quick Feet Drills Weightlifting	Week 2 No training prescribed rest or participate in light physical activity. i.e. basketball, biking, etc.
Week 3 NO WORKOUT REST	Week 3 **Kickers** Quick Feet Drills Weightlifting	Week 3 **Kick** 10 reps outside Game Winning Field Goals Workout Running Workout	Week 3 **Kickers** Quick Feet Drills Weightlifting	Week 3 **Kick** 10 reps outside Game Winning Field Goals Workout Running Workout	Week 3 **Kickers** Quick Feet Drills Weightlifting	Week 3 No training prescribed rest or participate in light physical activity. i.e. basketball, biking, etc.
Week 4 NO WORKOUT REST	Week 4 **Kickers** Quick Feet Drills Weightlifting	Week 4 NO WORKOUT REST	Week 4 **Kickers** Quick Feet Drills Weightlifting	Week 4 **Kick** 10 reps outside Game Winning Field Goals Workout Running Workout	Week 4 NO WORKOUT REST	Week 4 NO WORKOUT REST

High School KICKERS
PRE-SEASON SPEED and STRENGTH Training Program
July

MONDAY	TUESDAY	WEDNESDAY	THURSDAY	FRIDAY
Flexibility Agility Warm-up Dynamic Flexibility	**Flexibility** Agility Warm-up Dynamic Flexibility	**Flexibility** Agility Warm-up Dynamic Flexibility	**Flexibility** Agility Warm-up Dynamic Flexibility	**Flexibility** Agility Warm-up Dynamic Flexibility
Kicker Drills **1 set of 10** No Step Drill One Step Drill Quick Feet Full Approach Drill	**Kicker Drills** **1 set of 5** No Step Drill One Step Drill Quick Feet Full Approach Drill	**Kicker Drills** **1 set of 10** No Step Drill One Step Drill Quick Feet Full Approach Drill	**Kicker Drills** **1 set of 10** No Step Drill One Step Drill Quick Feet Full Approach Drill	**Kicker Drills** **1 set of 10** No Step Drill One Step Drill Quick Feet Full Approach Drill
Core Lifts **3 sets of 5** Squat Close Grip Bench Press	**Kicking Workout** 20 Kicks outside	**Core Lifts** **3 sets of 5** Cleans Deadlift	**Kicking Workout** 20 Kicks outside	**Core Lifts** **3 sets of 5** Lunges Bench Press
Auxiliary Lifts **2 sets of 8** Lat Pull Front Raises Lateral Raises Arm Curls Tricep Extension	**Running Workout** 2 x 220 yd sprints – ¾ speed 3 minute rest between each 4 x 110 yd sprints – ¾ speed 2 minute rest between each	**Auxiliary Lifts** **2 sets of 8** Glute Ham Raise Push Press Dips	**Running Workout** 2 x 220 yd sprints – ¾ speed 3 minute rest between each 4 x 110 yd sprints – ¾ speed 2 minute rest between each	**Auxiliary Lifts** **2 sets of 8** Lat Pulls Leg Extension Leg Curls Neck Arm Curls Tricep Extension

Agility Warm-up Routine
*15 yards – down and back using each movement
High knees
Shuffle
Carioca
Backpedal
Butt kicks
Power skips
Sprint

Dynamic Flexibility Routine
*10 yards – down and back using each movement
Tin soldiers
Walking Hamstring
Knee Tuck/Quad Pull
Front Lunges
Back Lunges
Spiderman

Kicker Workout Recording Sheet

Monday
July Week 1

Flexibility   ### Check when completed

Agility Warm-up   _____

Dynamic Flexibility   _____

Kicking Specific Drills   ### Check when completed

No-Step Swings   1 x 10 swings   _____

One-Step Swings   1 x 10 swings   _____

Quick Feet Full Approach Swings   1 x 10 swings   _____

Core Lifts   ### Weight Used

Squats   3 x 8 reps   _____

Close Grip Bench Press   3 x 8 reps   _____

Auxiliary Lifts   ### Weight Used

Lat Pulls   2 x 8 reps   _____

Front Raises (shoulders)   2 x 8 reps   _____

Lateral Raises (shoulders)   2 x 8 reps   _____

Arm Curls   2 x 8 reps   _____

Triceps Extensions   2 x 8 reps   _____

Notes
   1)   Use a weight you can complete all the repetitions comfortably meaning you could do one or
        two more at the end of the set.
   2)   When you could do more than two more repetitions on a set move the weight used up 5 pounds.
   3)   Rest only 1 minute between sets and no longer.

Kicking Workout Chart
Game Winning Field Goals

Left Hash	Middle	Right Hash	Kickoffs
1) __ 32 __	11) __ 35 __	21) __ 38 __	1) _____ , _____
2) __ 35 __	12) __ 40 __	22) __ 40 __	2) _____ , _____
3) __ 42 __	13) __ 43 __	23) __ 44 __	3) _____ , _____
4) _____	14) __ 45 __	24) _____	4) _____ , _____
5) _____	15) _____	25) _____	5) _____ , _____
6) _____	16) _____	26) _____	Hang Time, Distance
7) _____		**27)** _____	

Date: Tuesday, July Week 1

Field Goals: _____ - 10

Left Hash: _____ - 3   Middle: _____ - 4   Right Hash: _____ - 3

Kickoffs: 5

Kicker Workout Recording Sheet

Wednesday
July Week 1

Flexibility

Check when completed

Agility Warm-up   _____

Dynamic Flexibility   _____

Kicking Specific Drills

Check when completed

No-Step Swings	1 x 10 swings	_____
One-Step Swings	1 x 10 swings	_____
Quick Feet Full Approach Swings	1 x 10 swings	_____

Core Lifts

Weight Used

Power Cleans	3 x 8 reps	_____
Deadlift	3 x 8 reps	_____

Auxiliary Lifts

Weight Used

Glute Ham Raise	2 x 8 reps	_____
Push Press	2 x 8 reps	_____
Dips	2 x 8 reps	_____

Notes
1) Use a weight you can complete all the repetitions comfortably meaning you could do one or two more at the end of the set.
2) When you could do more than two more repetitions on a set move the weight used up 5 pounds.
3) Rest only 1 minute between sets and no longer.

Kicking Workout Chart
Game Winning Field Goals

Left Hash	Middle	Right Hash	Kickoffs
1) __ 32 __	11) __ 35 __	21) __ 38 __	1) _____, _____
2) __ 35 __	12) __ 40 __	22) __ 40 __	2) _____, _____
3) __ 42 __	13) __ 43 __	23) __ 44 __	3) _____, _____
4) _____	14) __ 45 __	24) _____	4) _____, _____
5) _____	15) _____	25) _____	5) _____,_____
6) _____	16) _____	26) _____	Hang Time, Distance
7) _____		27) _____	

Date: Thursday, July Week 1

Field Goals: _____ - 10

Left Hash: _____ - 3   Middle: _____ - 4   Right Hash: _____ - 3

Kickoffs: 5

Kicker Workout Recording Sheet

Friday
July Week 1

Flexibility   Check when completed

Agility Warm-up   _____

Dynamic Flexibility   _____

Kicking Specific Drills   Check when completed

No-Step Swings   1 x 10 swings   _____

One-Step Swings   1 x 10 swings   _____

Quick Feet Full Approach Swings   1 x 10 swings   _____

Core Lifts   Weight Used

Lunges   3 x 8 reps   _____

Bench Press   3 x 8 reps   _____

Auxiliary Lifts   Weight Used

Lat Pulls   2 x 8 reps   _____

Leg Extension   2 x 8 reps   _____

Leg Curls   2 x 8 reps   _____

Neck   2 x 8 reps   _____

Arm Curls   2 x 8 reps   _____

Triceps Extensions   2 x 8 reps   _____

Notes
1) Use a weight you can complete all the repetitions comfortably meaning you could do one or two more at the end of the set.
2) When you could do more than two more repetitions on a set move the weight used up 5 pounds.
3) Rest only 1 minute between sets and no longer

Weekly Kicking Chart Summary

Dates: July Week 1

Weekly Kicking Performance Summary

DISTANCE		Percent		Field Goal ACCURACY		Percent
20-24:	_____ - 0	0 %		Left Hash:	_____ - 6	_____
25-29:	_____ - 0	0 %		Middle:	_____ - 8	_____
30-34:	_____ - 2	_____		Right Hash:	_____ - 6	_____
35-39:	_____ - 6	_____				
40-44:	_____ - 10	_____		**KICKOFFS**		
45-49:	_____ - 2	_____		Number:	10	
50+:	_____ - 0	0 %		Avg. Hang Time:	_____	
				Avg. Distance:	_____	

TOTALS

Field Goals: _____ - 20

FG % _____

L = Left Hash
M = Middle
R = Right Hash

*Plot all this weeks field goals on the goal posts.
Use L for the left hash field goals, use R for the right hash field goals and M for field goals from the middle.

Kicker Workout Recording Sheet

Monday
July Week 2

Flexibility   ### Check when completed

Agility Warm-up   _____

Dynamic Flexibility   _____

Kicking Specific Drills   ### Check when completed

No-Step Swings   1 x 10 swings   _____

One-Step Swings   1 x 10 swings   _____

Quick Feet Full Approach Swings   1 x 10 swings   _____

Core Lifts   ### Weight Used

Squats   3 x 8 reps   _____

Close Grip Bench Press   3 x 8 reps   _____

Auxiliary Lifts   ### Weight Used

Lat Pulls   2 x 8 reps   _____

Front Raises (shoulders)   2 x 8 reps   _____

Lateral Raises (shoulders)   2 x 8 reps   _____

Arm Curls   2 x 8 reps   _____

Triceps Extensions   2 x 8 reps   _____

Notes
1) Use a weight you can complete all the repetitions comfortably meaning you could do one or two more at the end of the set.
2) When you could do more than two more repetitions on a set move the weight used up 5 pounds.
3) Rest only 1 minute between sets and no longer.

Kicking Workout Chart
Game Winning Field Goals

Left Hash	Middle	Right Hash	Kickoffs
1) __ 32 __	11) __ 35 __	21) __ 38 __	1) _____ , _____
2) __ 35 __	12) __ 40 __	22) __ 40 __	2) _____ , _____
3) __ 42 __	13) __ 43 __	23) __ 44 __	3) _____ , _____
4) _____	14) __ 45 __	24) _____	4) _____ , _____
5) _____	15) _____	25) _____	5) _____ , _____
6) _____	16) _____	26) _____	Hang Time, Distance
7) _____		27) _____	

Date: Tuesday, July Week 2

Field Goals: _____ - 10

Left Hash: _____ - 3   Middle: _____ - 4   Right Hash: _____ - 3

Kickoffs: 5

Kicker Workout Recording Sheet

Wednesday
July Week 2

Flexibility   ### Check when completed

Agility Warm-up   _____

Dynamic Flexibility   _____

Kicking Specific Drills   ### Check when completed

No-Step Swings   1 x 10 swings   _____

One-Step Swings   1 x 10 swings   _____

Quick Feet Full Approach Swings   1 x 10 swings   _____

Core Lifts   ### Weight Used

Power Cleans   3 x 8 reps   _____

Deadlift   3 x 8 reps   _____

Auxiliary Lifts   ### Weight Used

Glute Ham Raise   2 x 8 reps   _____

Push Press   2 x 8 reps   _____

Dips   2 x 8 reps   _____

Notes
1) Use a weight you can complete all the repetitions comfortably meaning you could do one or two more at the end of the set.
2) When you could do more than two more repetitions on a set move the weight used up 5 pounds.
3) Rest only 1 minute between sets and no longer.

Game Winning Field Goals

Left Hash	Middle	Right Hash	Kickoffs
1) __ 32 __	11) __ 35 __	21) __ 38 __	1) _____, _____
2) __ 35 __	12) __ 40 __	22) __ 40 __	2) _____, _____
3) __ 42 __	13) __ 43 __	23) __ 44 __	3) _____, _____
4) _____	14) __ 45 __	24) _____	4) _____, _____
5) _____	15) _____	25) _____	5) _____,_____
6) _____	16) _____	26) _____	Hang Time, Distance
7) _____		27) _____	

Date: Thursday, July Week 2

Field Goals: _____ - 10

Left Hash: _____ - 3   Middle: _____ - 4   Right Hash: _____ - 3

Kickoffs: 5

Kicker Workout Recording Sheet

Friday
July Week 2

Flexibility		Check when completed
Agility Warm-up		_____
Dynamic Flexibility		_____

Kicking Specific Drills		Check when completed
No-Step Swings	1 x 10 swings	_____
One-Step Swings	1 x 10 swings	_____
Quick Feet Full Approach Swings	1 x 10 swings	_____

Core Lifts		Weight Used
Lunges	3 x 8 reps	_____
Bench Press	3 x 8 reps	_____

Auxiliary Lifts		Weight Used
Lat Pulls	2 x 8 reps	_____
Leg Extension	2 x 8 reps	_____
Leg Curls	2 x 8 reps	_____
Neck	2 x 8 reps	_____
Arm Curls	2 x 8 reps	_____
Triceps Extensions	2 x 8 reps	_____

Notes
1) Use a weight you can complete all the repetitions comfortably meaning you could do one or two more at the end of the set.
2) When you could do more than two more repetitions on a set move the weight used up 5 pounds.
3) Rest only 1 minute between sets and no longer

Weekly Kicking Chart Summary

Dates: July Week 2

Weekly Kicking Performance Summary

DISTANCE		Percent	Field Goal ACCURACY		Percent
20-24: _____	- 0	0 %	Left Hash: _____	- 6	_____
25-29: _____	- 0	0 %	Middle: _____	- 8	_____
30-34: _____	- 2	_____	Right Hash: _____	- 6	_____
35-39: _____	- 6	_____			
40-44: _____	- 10	_____	**KICKOFFS**		
45-49: _____	- 2	_____	Number: 10		
50+: _____	- 0	0 %	Avg. Hang Time: _____		
			Avg. Distance: _____		

TOTALS

Field Goals: _____ - 20

FG % _____

L = Left Hash
M = Middle
R = Right Hash

*Plot all this weeks field goals on the goal posts.
Use L for the left hash field goals, use R for the right hash field goals and M for field goals from the middle.

Kicker Workout Recording Sheet

Monday
July Week 3

Flexibility

Check when completed

Agility Warm-up   _____

Dynamic Flexibility   _____

Kicking Specific Drills

Check when completed

No-Step Swings	1 x 10 swings	_____
One-Step Swings	1 x 10 swings	_____
Quick Feet Full Approach Swings	1 x 10 swings	_____

Core Lifts

Weight Used

Squats	3 x 8 reps	_____
Close Grip Bench Press	3 x 8 reps	_____

Auxiliary Lifts

Weight Used

Lat Pulls	2 x 8 reps	_____
Front Raises (shoulders)	2 x 8 reps	_____
Lateral Raises (shoulders)	2 x 8 reps	_____
Arm Curls	2 x 8 reps	_____
Triceps Extensions	2 x 8 reps	_____

Notes
1) Use a weight you can complete all the repetitions comfortably meaning you could do one or two more at the end of the set.
2) When you could do more than two more repetitions on a set move the weight used up 5 pounds.
3) Rest only 1 minute between sets and no longer.

Game Winning Field Goals

Left Hash	Middle	Right Hash	Kickoffs
1) __ 32 __	11) __ 35 __	21) __ 38 __	1) _____, _____
2) __ 35 __	12) __ 40 __	22) __ 40 __	2) _____, _____
3) __ 42 __	13) __ 43 __	23) __ 44 __	3) _____, _____
4) _____	14) __ 45 __	24) _____	4) _____, _____
5) _____	15) _____	25) _____	5) _____,_____
6) _____	16) _____	26) _____	Hang Time, Distance
7) _____		27) _____	

Date: Tuesday, July Week 3

Field Goals: _____ - 10

Left Hash: _____ - 3   Middle: _____ - 4   Right Hash: _____ - 3

Kickoffs: 5

Kicker Workout Recording Sheet

Wednesday
July Week 3

Flexibility   ### Check when completed

Agility Warm-up   _____

Dynamic Flexibility   _____

Kicking Specific Drills   ### Check when completed

No-Step Swings   1 x 10 swings   _____

One-Step Swings   1 x 10 swings   _____

Quick Feet Full Approach Swings   1 x 10 swings   _____

Core Lifts   ### Weight Used

Power Cleans   3 x 8 reps   _____

Deadlift   3 x 8 reps   _____

Auxiliary Lifts   ### Weight Used

Glute Ham Raise   2 x 8 reps   _____

Push Press   2 x 8 reps   _____

Dips   2 x 8 reps   _____

Notes
1) Use a weight you can complete all the repetitions comfortably meaning you could do one or two more at the end of the set.
2) When you could do more than two more repetitions on a set move the weight used up 5 pounds.
3) Rest only 1 minute between sets and no longer.

Game Winning Field Goals

Left Hash	Middle	Right Hash	Kickoffs
1) __ 32 __	11) __ 35 __	21) __ 38 __	1) _____, _____
2) __ 35 __	12) __ 40 __	22) __ 40 __	2) _____, _____
3) __ 42 __	13) __ 43 __	23) __ 44 __	3) _____, _____
4) _____	14) __ 45 __	24) _____	4) _____, _____
5) _____	15) _____	25) _____	5) _____, _____
6) _____	16) _____	26) _____	Hang Time, Distance
7) _____		27) _____	

Date: Thursday, July Week 3

Field Goals: _____ - 10

Left Hash: _____ - 3 Middle: _____ - 4   Right Hash: _____ - 3

Kickoffs: 5

Kicker Workout Recording Sheet

Friday
July Week 3

Flexibility		Check when completed
Agility Warm-up		_____
Dynamic Flexibility		_____

Kicking Specific Drills		Check when completed
No-Step Swings	1 x 10 swings	_____
One-Step Swings	1 x 10 swings	_____
Quick Feet Full Approach Swings	1 x 10 swings	_____

Core Lifts		Weight Used
Lunges	3 x 8 reps	_____
Bench Press	3 x 8 reps	_____

Auxiliary Lifts		Weight Used
Lat Pulls	2 x 8 reps	_____
Leg Extension	2 x 8 reps	_____
Leg Curls	2 x 8 reps	_____
Neck	2 x 8 reps	_____
Arm Curls	2 x 8 reps	_____
Triceps Extensions	2 x 8 reps	_____

Notes
1) Use a weight you can complete all the repetitions comfortably meaning you could do one or two more at the end of the set.
2) When you could do more than two more repetitions on a set move the weight used up 5 pounds.
3) Rest only 1 minute between sets and no longer

July
Weekly Kicking Chart Summary

Dates: July Week 3

Weekly Kicking Performance Summary

DISTANCE		**Percent**		**Field Goal ACCURACY**		**Percent**
20-24:	_____ - 0	0 %		Left Hash:	_____ - 6	_____
25-29:	_____ - 0	0 %		Middle:	_____ - 8	_____
30-34:	_____ - 2	_____		Right Hash:	_____ - 6	_____
35-39:	_____ - 6	_____				
40-44:	_____ - 10	_____		**KICKOFFS**		
45-49:	_____ - 2	_____		Number:	10	
50+:	_____ - 0	0 %		Avg. Hang Time:	_____	
				Avg. Distance:	_____	

TOTALS

Field Goals: _____ - 20

FG % _____

L = Left Hash
M = Middle
R = Right Hash

*Plot all this weeks field goals on the goal posts.
Use L for the left hash field goals, use R for the right hash field goals and M for field goals from the middle.

Kicker Workout Recording Sheet

Monday
July Week 4

Flexibility   Check when completed

Agility Warm-up   _____

Dynamic Flexibility   _____

Kicking Specific Drills   Check when completed

No-Step Swings   1 x 10 swings   _____

One-Step Swings   1 x 10 swings   _____

Quick Feet Full Approach Swings   1 x 10 swings   _____

Core Lifts   Weight Used

Squats   3 x 8 reps   _____

Close Grip Bench Press   3 x 8 reps   _____

Auxiliary Lifts   Weight Used

Lat Pulls   2 x 8 reps   _____

Front Raises (shoulders) 2 x 8 reps   _____

Lateral Raises (shoulders)   2 x 8 reps   _____

Arm Curls   2 x 8 reps   _____

Triceps Extensions   2 x 8 reps   _____

Notes
1) Use a weight you can complete all the repetitions comfortably meaning you could do one or two more at the end of the set.
2) When you could do more than two more repetitions on a set move the weight used up 5 pounds.
3) Rest only 1 minute between sets and no longer.

No Workout

REST

Kicker Workout Recording Sheet

Wednesday
July Week 4

Flexibility   ### Check when completed

Agility Warm-up   15 yards down and back   _____

Dynamic Flexibility   10 yards down and back   _____

Kicking Specific Drills   ### Check when completed

No-Step Swings   1 x 10 swings   _____

One-Step Swings   1 x 10 swings   _____

Quick Feet Full Approach Swings   1 x 10 swings   _____

Core Lifts   ### Weight Used

Power Cleans   3 x 8 reps   _____

Deadlift   3 x 8 reps   _____

Auxiliary Lifts   ### Weight Used

Glute Ham Raise   2 x 8 reps   _____

Push Press   2 x 8 reps   _____

Dips   2 x 8 reps   _____

Notes
1) Use a weight you can complete all the repetitions comfortably meaning you could do one or two more at the end of the set.
2) When you could do more than two more repetitions on a set move the weight used up 5 pounds.
3) Rest only 1 minute between sets and no longer.

Game Winning Field Goals

Left Hash	Middle	Right Hash	Kickoffs
1) __ 32 __	11) __ 35 __	21) __ 38 __	1) _____, _____
2) __ 35 __	12) __ 40 __	22) __ 40 __	2) _____, _____
3) __ 42 __	13) __ 43 __	23) __ 44 __	3) _____, _____
4) _____	14) __ 45 __	24) _____	4) _____, _____
5) _____	15) _____	25) _____	5) _____, _____
6) _____	16) _____	26) _____	Hang Time, Distance
7) _____		27) _____	

Date: Thursday, July Week 4

Field Goals: _____ - 10

Left Hash: _____ - 3   Middle: _____ - 4   Right Hash: _____ - 3

Kickoffs: 5

194

No Workout

REST

July
Weekly Kicking Chart Summary

Dates: July Week 4

Weekly Kicking Performance Summary

DISTANCE		Percent	Field Goal ACCURACY		Percent
20-24:	_____ - 0	0 %	Left Hash:	_____ - 3	_____
25-29:	_____ - 0	0 %	Middle:	_____ - 4	_____
30-34:	_____ - 1	_____	Right Hash:	_____ - 3	_____
35-39:	_____ - 3	_____			
40-44:	_____ - 5	_____	**KICKOFFS**		
45-49:	_____ - 1	_____	Number:	5	
50+:	_____ - 0	0 %	Avg. Hang Time:	_____	
			Avg. Distance:	_____	

TOTALS

Field Goals: _____ - 10

FG % _____

L = Left Hash
M = Middle
R = Right Hash

*Plot all this weeks field goals on the goal posts.
Use L for the left hash field goals, use R for the right hash field goals and M for field goals from the middle.

July
MONTHLY Kicking Chart Summary

Dates: July Weeks 1 - 4

MONTHLY Kicking Performance Summary

DISTANCE		Percent	Field Goal ACCURACY		Percent
20-24:	_____ - 0	0 %	Left Hash:	_____ - 21	_____
25-29:	_____ - 0	0 %	Middle:	_____ - 28	_____
30-34:	_____ - 7	_____	Right Hash:	_____ - 21	_____
35-39:	_____ - 21	_____			
40-44:	_____ - 35	_____	**KICKOFFS**		
45-49:	_____ - 7	_____	Number: 35		
50+:	_____ - 0	0 %	Avg. Hang Time: _____		
			Avg. Distance: _____		

TOTALS

Field Goals: _____ - 70

FG % _____

April - July

5 Month Summary

Kicking Workout Charts

April - July
MONTHLY Kicking Chart Summary

Dates: April– July

5 MONTH's Kicking Performance Summary

DISTANCE	Percent	Field Goal ACCURACY	Percent
20-24: _____ - 0	0 %	Left Hash: _____ - 291	_____
25-29: _____ - 0	0 %	Middle: _____ - 258	_____
30-34: _____ - 127	_____	Right Hash: _____ - 291	_____
35-39: _____ - 255	_____		
40-44: _____ - 269	_____	**KICKOFFS**	
45-49: _____ - 142	_____	Number: 230	
50+: _____ - 57	_____	Avg. Hang Time: _____	
		Avg. Distance: _____	

TOTALS

Field Goals: _____ - 850

FG % _____

*add each MONTHLY Kicking Chart summary to get the totals for this chart

Appendix

Charting System
Quick Feet Drills Coaching Points
Agilities, Dynamic Flexibility and Stretching

Charting System

For

Kickers

Kicking Workout Chart

Game Winning Field Goals

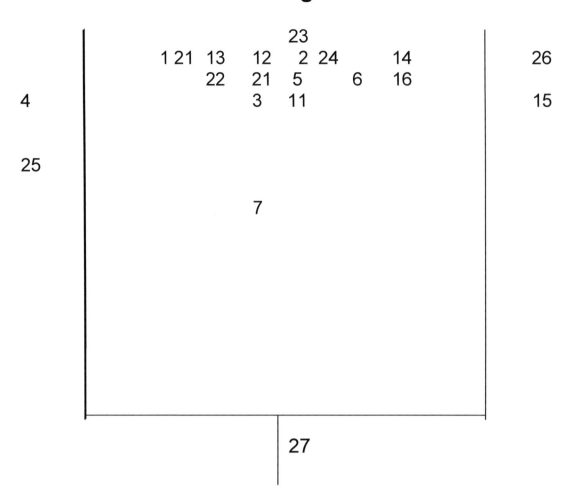

	Left Hash		Middle		Right Hash		Kickoffs
1)	__ 30 __	11)	__ 30 __	21)	__ 30 __	1)	-2, 3.85
2)	__ 32 __	12)	__ 32 __	22)	__ 32 __	2)	GL, 3.97
3)	__ 35 __	13)	__ 35 __	23)	__ 35 __	3)	-5, 4.12
4)	__ 38 __	14)	__ 38 __	24)	__ 38 __	4)	+4, 3.88
5)	__ 40 __	15)	__ 40 __	25)	__ 40 __	5)	-6, 3.69
6)	__ 42 __	16)	__ 42 __	26)	__ 42 __		Hang Time, Distance
7)	__ 45 __			27)	__ 45 __		

Date: Monday, 10/12/14

Field Goals: 15 - 20

Left Hash: 6 - 7   **Middle:** 5 - 6   **Right Hash**: 4 - 7

Kickoffs: 5

Game Week 1
Weekly Kicking Summary Chart

Dates: 10/12/14

Weekly Kicking Performance Summary

DISTANCE		Percent		Field Goal ACCURACY		Percent
20-24:	___ - 0	0 %		Left Hash: 6 - 7		86%
25-29:	___ - 0	0 %		Middle: 5 - 6		83%
30-34:	6 - 6	100%		Right Hash: 4 - 7		57%
35-39:	5 - 6	83%				
40-44:	3 - 6	50%		**KICKOFFS**		
45-49:	1 - 2	50%		Number: 15		
50+:	___ - 0	___ %		Avg. Hang Time: 3.90		
				Avg. Distance: 62 yards (-2 yd deep)		

TOTALS

Field Goals: 15 - 20

FG % : 75%

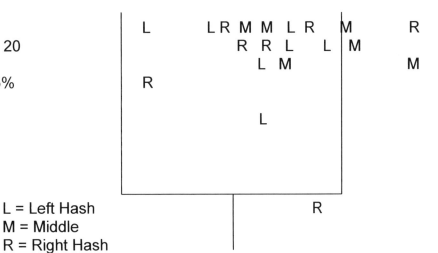

L = Left Hash
M = Middle
R = Right Hash

*Plot all this weeks field goals on the goal posts.
Use **L** for the left hash field goals, use **R** for the right hash field goals and **M** for field goals from the middle.

Kicking Recording Examples

The following pictures represent the most common types of marks made for charting field goal kicks. The key thing to remember is to simply <u>place the number of the kick on the chart where it went through or by the goal post</u>. By charting the location of the balls flight through the goal posts, the coach can detect strengths and weaknesses in his kicker.

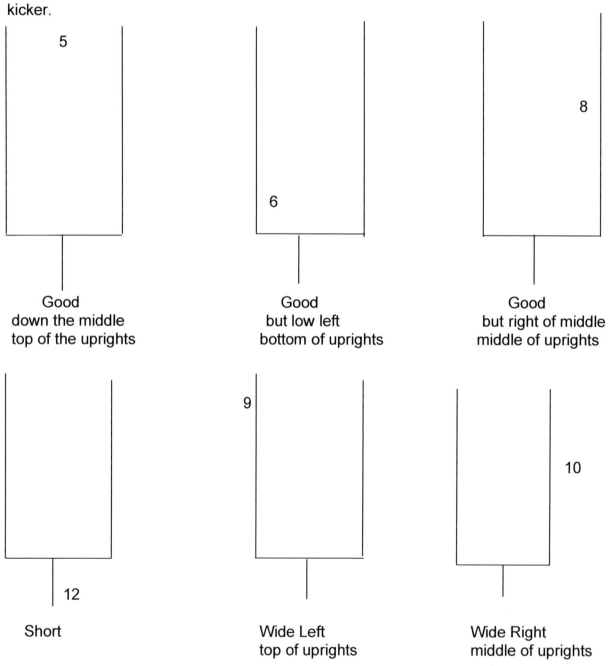

Good	Good	Good
down the middle	but low left	but right of middle
top of the uprights	bottom of uprights	middle of uprights

Short	Wide Left	Wide Right
	top of uprights	middle of uprights

Interpreting the Charts

The ability to interpret the kicking charts accurately is essential to fully utilizing the advantages of charting a kicker. <u>Recognition of the chart patterns</u> can tell you whether the <u>kicker is pulling the ball left</u>, <u>pushing the ball right</u>, <u>which hash mark he is better from</u>, and <u>how consistent he is in contacting the ball</u>.

Remember how many games are decided by three points or less. Take the time to chart and interpret your kickers data and you will increase his chances of making that winning kick!

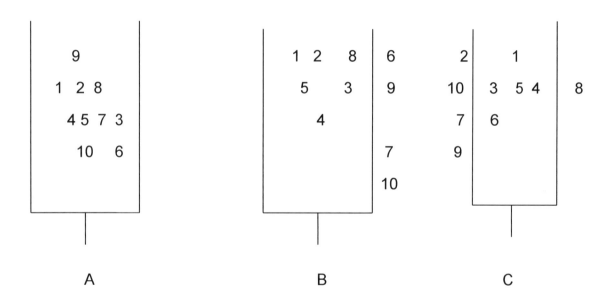

Kick Chart Pattern Interpretations

- **Chart A** - A kick chart that has this type of pattern indicates a <u>kicker who is accurate and consistent</u>. Notice the closeness of the numbers to the center of the goal posts with only two kicks, 3 and 6, which are off center. This tells the coach that the <u>kicker is making good contact with the ball</u> and is accurate from the range charted.

- **Chart B** - This pattern of kicks indicates that the <u>kicker is pushing the ball to the right</u> upon contact. The majority of the charted kicks are to the right of the center of the goal posts indicating that the kicker may be <u>planting too close to the ball,</u> <u>not aligning properly before approaching the ball</u> or <u>not accelerating and swinging through the ball.</u>

- **Chart C** - With most of the charted kicks to the left of the center of the goal posts, this pattern denotes that the <u>kicker is pulling the ball to the left</u>. This is an indicator of <u>swinging too fast and hard at the ball,</u> <u>not releasing his hips up and toward the target,</u> or <u>pointing the plant foot to the left of the target</u>.

Kickers Quick Feet Drills
Coaching Points

1. **NO Step Drill**
   a. Foot in "plant box"
   b. Tall, athletic position, weight on ball of plant foot
   c. Pull kicking foot off the ground remaining balanced and stable in upper body
   d. Pull kicking foot heel back to the butt cheek
   e. Transfer weight from heel to toe and push UP through the contact zone
   f. SNAP the kicking leg downward
   g. ACCELERATE through contact
   h. Finish balanced-square to target, no leaning left, right or backward

2. **ONE Step Drill**
   a. Start 1 ½ yds behind and 1 yd over from the spot of the ball
   b. Put kicking foot forward with toe pointing at back of tee
   c. Tall, athletic position, weight on ball of plant foot
   d. Drive off the first step "ACCELERATE"
   e. Place plant foot in the box, toe straight at target
   f. Hit the ground with a heel-toe-UP off plant step
   g. Maintain balance and posture throughout the swing while going FULL SPEED
   h. Finish balanced-square to target, no leaning left, right or backward

3. **FULL Approach On Air – not kicking the ball**
   a. Start 3 yds behind and 1 ½ yds over from the ball spot
   b. Put kicking foot forward with toe pointing at back of tee
   c. Tall, athletic position, weight on ball of plant foot
   d. Push off non-kicking foot to get your body moving -"0-60mph BURST"
   e. On approach, pick feet up and down like "PISTONS" to generate leg speed and remain balanced and stable in upper body throughout approach
   f. Drive off the first step "ACCELERATE"
   g. Place plant foot in the box, toe straight at target
   h. Hit the ground with a heel-toe-UP off plant step
   i. Maintain balance and posture throughout the swing while going FULL SPEED
   j. Finish balanced-square to target, no leaning left, right or backward

4. **FULL Kicks**
   a. Will contacting the ball change your mindset or mechanics?
   b. Be AGGRESSIVE and ATTACK the football
   c. Be a GREAT ball striker
   d. The FULL Kick mechanics should be the same as the FULL Approach
   e. Start 2 ½ yds behind and 1 ½ yds over from the ball spot
   f. Put kicking foot forward with toe pointing at back of tee
   g. Tall, athletic position, weight on ball of plant foot
   h. Push off non-kicking foot to get your body moving -"0-60mph BURST"
   i. On approach, pick feet up and down like "PISTONS" to generate leg speed and remain balanced and stable in upper body throughout approach
   j. Drive off the first step "ACCELERATE"
   k. Place plant foot in the box, toe straight at target
   l. Hit the ground with a heel-toe-UP off plant step
   m. Maintain balance and posture throughout the swing while going FULL SPEED
   n. Finish balanced-square to target, no leaning left, right or backward

Agilities
Dynamic Flexibility
and Stretching Routine

Agilities   15 yards – down and back using each movement
High knees,
Shuffle
Carioca
Backpedal
Butt kicks
Power skips
Sprint

Dynamic Flexibility   10 yards – down and back using each movement
Tin Soldiers,
Walking Hamstrings
Knee Tuck/ Quad Pull
Front Lunges
Back Lunges
Spiderman

Stretching
*All stretches are done twice through. Each stretch is held for 10 seconds.

10 one count jumping jacks
Leg V
  - Right Leg stretch
  - Left Leg stretch
Butterfly
Right Leg Pretzel
Left Leg Pretzel
Cobra (lie on stomach and arch back)
Push ups (10)
Right Knee Hip Flex
Left Knee Hip Flex
Left Calf Stretch
Left Achilles Stretch (bend-the-knee)
Right Calf Stretch
Right Achilles Stretch (bend-the-knee)
Over the head (hands crossed, arms over the head)
Behind the back (hands behind the back)
10 one count jumping jack

For additional coaching educational materials

by Coach Bill Renner

visit:

www.billrennerfootball.com

Made in the USA
Middletown, DE
05 December 2016